*Python Programming &
Machine Learning With
Python Bundle Pack 2
Manuscripts in 1 BOOK*

*Best Illustrated Guide For
Beginners & Intermediates :
The Future Is Here!*

Table of Contents

FREE E-BOOK DOWNLOAD :

http://bit.ly/2yJsyq4

or

http://pragmaticsolutionstech.co
m/

Use the link above to get instant access to the bestselling E-Book **Data Analytics' Guide For Beginners**

Chapter 1

Introduction

Python is a loosely typed object oriented programming language used to perform variety of programming tasks ranging from web development and desktop application development to data science and machine learning etc. Owing to its simplicity of syntax and ease of learning, Python has become one of the leading programming languages of the world. Python was created by Guido van Rossum in late 1980s. This book provides a gateway to in-depth Python programming.

Why Python?

There are several advantages of learning Python. Some of them are as follows:

- **Easy to learn**

Python is one of the easiest languages to learn owing to its super simple syntax and loose typing. Unlike other languages, you don't have to learn how to use myriads of bracket types in order specify code blocks. You also don't get end of line semicolon errors. Finally, you also don't have to specify the type of variable while storing data in it. These points might sound trivial to expert programmers, but for a person new to programming they are serious turn-offs.

- **Open Source and Large Developer Community**

Python is an open source language which means it can be used to develop, share and distribute applications for commercial as well as non-commercial purposes without any copyright infringements. Furthermore, Python's large developer community makes it easier to lookup for solutions to the problem.

- **Support for Web development**

Python can be used for developing websites. In fact there are some very good Python frameworks such as Django and Flask that make server side web development much easier and robust.

- **Used for Data Science Machine Learning**

You would have heard the term "Data is the future." If data is really the future, then Python is surely the language to learn since most of the data science and machine learning are currently being implemented via Python. There are several machine learning and deep learning libraries such as Sklearn, Tensorflow, Keras that made it simple to develop complex machine learning models.

Important Features of Python

Following are some of the most important features of Python:

- **Source code to Byte code**

Python source code is compiled directly to byte code without any intermediate steps. This makes Python script run on multiple platforms without requiring any additional tool.

- **Object Oriented**

Python is 100% object oriented language. Everything in Python is an object. Furthermore, python provides an easy way to create new objects via classes.

- **Support for C/C++ Extension**

Python code can be further extended in C and C++. Speed of a Python program can be significantly increased this way.

- **Dynamic Language**

Python is a dynamic language. Values, instead of variables are bound to types.

Furthermore, Method and function lookup is performed at runtime.

- **Automatic Garbage Collection**

Garbage collection is performed automatically in Python. However, "gc" module can be used to perform garbage collection at any given time.

- **Highly Structured Language**

Statements, functions, classes, modules and packages and most importantly Python's indentation based syntax allows developers to write highly structured and readable code.

- **Fast and Maintainable Compared to Other Languages**

In comparison with other compiled languages, Python is faster, more structured and more maintainable.

About the Book

This book is aimed towards providing in-depth yet simple insight into Python programming language. The book is geared towards beginner as well as advanced readers. The book helps beginners get their feet wet with practical Python. On the other hand, it can be used by expert users as a reference to different basic and advanced Python concepts.

All the important Python concepts have been grouped into chapters. A chapter contains theoretical information about particular Python concepts along with their implementation in the form of Python script. To get the most of this book, readers are suggested to first thoroughly understand the concept and then practice the code.

What's next?

In the next chapter we will set up the environment required to run python script. We will install different software needed to run the scripts in this book. Happy Coding!!!

Chapter 2

Environment Setup

In this chapter we will install the software that we are going to use to run our Python programs. There are several options available in this regard. You can simply install core Python and use a text editor like notepad to write Python programs. These programs can then be run via command line utilities. The other option is to install an Integrated Develop Environment (IDE) for Python. IDE provides a complete programming environment including Python installation, Editors and debugging tools. Most of the advanced programmers take the IDE route for Python development. We are also going to take the same route.

Anaconda is the IDE that we are going to use throughout this book. Anaconda is light, easy to install and comes with variety of development tools. Anaconda has its own command line utility to install third party software. And the good thing is that with Anaconda, you don't have to separately install Python environment.

Downloading and Installing Anaconda

Follow these steps to download and install anaconda. In this section we will show the process of installing Anaconda for windows. The installation process remains almost same for Linux and Mac.

1- Go to the following URL https://www.anaconda.com/download/
2- You will be presented with the following webpage. Select Python 3.6 version as this is currently the latest version of Python. Click the "Download" button to download the

executable file. It takes 2-3 minutes to download the file depending upon the speed of your internet.

3- Once the executable file is downloaded, go to the download folder and run the executable. The name of the executable file should be similar to "Anaconda3-5.1.0-Windows-x86_64." When you run the file you will see installation wizard like the one in the following screenshot. Click "Next" button.

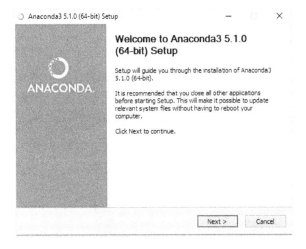

4- "License Agreement" dialogue box will appear. Read the license agreement and Click "I Agree" button.

5- From the "Select Installation Type" dialogue box, check the "Just Me" radio button and click "Next" button as shown in the following screenshot.

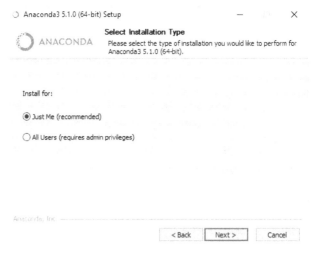

6- Choose the installation directory (Default is preferred) from the "Choose Install Location" dialogue box and click "Next" button. You should have around 3 GB of free space in your installation directory.

Anaconda3 5.1.0 (64-bit) Setup — □ ✕

Choose Install Location
Choose the folder in which to install Anaconda3 5.1.0 (64-bit).

Setup will install Anaconda3 5.1.0 (64-bit) in the following folder. To install in a different folder, click Browse and select another folder. Click Next to continue.

Destination Folder

C:\Users\Mani\Anaconda3   Browse...

Space required: 2.5GB
Space available: 148.5GB

Anaconda, Inc.

< Back   Next >   Cancel

7- From the "Advanced Installation Options" dialogue box, select the second checkbox "Register Anaconda as my default Python 3.6" and click the "Install" button as shown in the following screenshot.

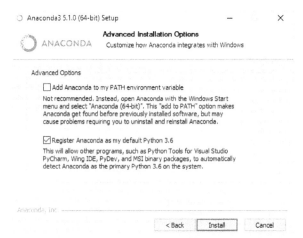

The installation process will start which can take some time to complete. Sit back and enjoy a cup of coffee.

8- Once the installation completes, click the "Next" button as shown below.

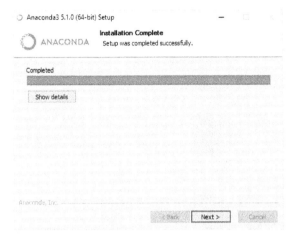

9- "Microsoft Visual Studio Code Installation" window appear, click "Skip" button.

10- Congratulations, you have installed Anaconda. Uncheck the both the checkboxes on the dialogue box that appears and "Finish" button.

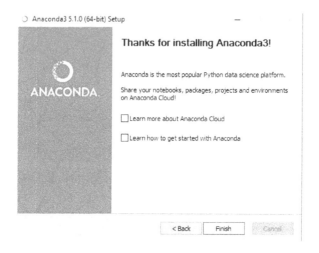

Running your First Program

We have installed environment required to run Python scripts. Now is the time to run our first program. With Anaconda, you have several ways to do so. We will see two of those in this section.

Go to your window search box and type "Anaconda Navigator" and then select the "Anaconda Navigator" application as shown below:

Anaconda Navigator
Desktop app

Folders

anaconda_navigator - in site-packages

anaconda_navigator - in site-packages

anaconda_navigator-1.7.0-py3.6.egg-info - in site-packages

anaconda_navigator-1.7.0-py3.6.egg-info - in site-packages

anaconda-navigator-1.7.0-py36_0

Search suggestions

$\mathcal{P}$ Anaconda Navigator - See web results 〉

$\mathcal{P}$ anaconda navigator youtube 〉

$\mathcal{P}$ anaconda navigator windows 〉

$\mathcal{P}$ anaconda navigator download 〉

$\mathcal{P}$ anaconda navigator app 〉

$\mathcal{P}$ Anaconda Navigator

Anaconda Navigator Dashboard will appear that looks like this.

Note: It takes some time for Anaconda Navigator to start, so be patient.

From the dashboard, you can see all of the tools available to develop your python applications. In this book we will mostly use "Jupyter Notebook" (second from top). Though in this chapter we shall also see how to run python script via "Spyder".

Running Scripts via Jupyter Notebook

Jupyter notebook runs in your default browser. From the navigator, launch "Jupyter Notebook" (Second option from the top).

Another way to launch Jupyter is by typing "Jupyter Notebook" in the search box and selecting the "Jupyter Notebook" application from the start menu as shown below:

Jupyter Notebook
Desktop app

Folders

jupyter_notebook_config.d - in jupyter

jupyter_notebook_config.d - in jupyter

Documents

jupyter-notebook-script

jupyter_notebook_config

Search suggestions

jupyter notebook - See web results 〉

jupyter notebook download 〉

jupyter notebook login 〉

jupyter notebook online 〉

jupyter notebook app 〉

jupyter notebook images 〉

jupyter notebook

Jupyter notebook will launch in a new tab of your default browser.

To create a new notebook, click "new" button at the top-right corner of the Jupyter notebook dashboard. From dropdown, select "Python 3."

You will see new Python 3 notebook that looks like this:

Jupyter notebook consists of cells. Python script is written inside these cells. Let's print hello world using Jupyter notebook. In the first cell of the notebook enter "print('hello world') and press CTRL+ ENTER. The script in the first cell will be executed as shown below:

The "print" function prints the string passed to it as parameter, in the output. To create a new cell, click the "+" button from the top left menu as shown below:

You can write Python script in the new cell and press CTRL + ENTER to execute it.

Running Scripts via Spyder

While Jupyter notebook is a good place to start writing Python programs, once you get comfortable with Python, you should move to Spyder IDE. Spyder allows us to directly create Python files. Spyder is similar to more conventional text editors with options to Run file, Run piece of code, debug code etc.

Just like Jupyter notebook, you can run Spyder from Anaconda Navigator or directly from Start Menu. You will be presented with the following interface once you run Spyder.

On the left side of the Spyder interface, you can see text editor; this is where you enter your script. On the bottom right you have console window. You can directly execute scripts in the console window. Furthermore, the output of the code written in the editor also appears in the console window. Let's write hello world program in Spyder.

To run script in Python you have two options. You can either click the green triangle from the top menu or you can select the piece of code you want to execute and press CTRL + ENTER from the keyboard. You will see the output in the console window.

What's next?

In this chapter we saw the process of setting up the environment required to run python programs. We wrote our first python program in two different editors. In the next chapter we will start our discussion about Python syntax. Happy Coding!!!

Chapter 3

Python Syntax

To write python code, you need to follow some rules. In programming terms, these rules are collectively called syntax. Python's unique syntax is one of the reasons that novice programmers find it easy to learn and program. In this chapter we shall study python syntax in detail.

Simple Statements

Unlike most of the other object oriented programming languages, Python doesn't require a semi colon at the end of the statement if there is only single statement in the line. In case if you want to write multiple python statements on one line (Which is highly not recommended), you have to separate them with semi-colon. Take a look at the following example.

Here we write two Python statements on two separate lines. We don't need semicolon.

```
print ("Welcome to Python")
```

```
print ("It is fun learning
Python")
```

When you execute the above statement, you will see following output:

```
Welcome to Python
It is fun learning Python
```

Now let's write two statements on one line separated by semi colon:

```
print ("Welcome to Python") ;
print ("It is fun learning
Python")
```

The output of the above script will be same since they actually are two statements even if they are written on one line.

You can also write a python statement that spans multiple lines. To do so, you have to append backward slash at the end of the line. Backward slash denotes that the statement continues to the next line. Take a look at the following script:

```
sum = 10 + 20 + \
```

```
    30 + 40 + \
    50

print(sum)
```

Code Blocks and Indentation

Indentation is one of the most striking features of Python syntax. In almost all of the other programming languages, braces are used to specify the scope of the code block. In Python, indentations specify the scope of the code block. Look at the following code snippet.

```
if 10 > 3:
    print("This is inside if block")
    print("This is also inside if block")


print("This is outside if block")
```

```
if 10 < 3:
    print("This is inside if
block")
    print("This is also inside
if block")
```

In the script above, the 'if' block evaluates if 10 is greater than 3, and then executes next two print statements that are indented 4 tabs to the right (which is standard). The statements indented are part of the "if block". After that, statement outside the 'if' block executes. The second if block evaluates if 10 is less than 3, which returns false. Therefore the statements that are part of the second 'if' block, indented to the right, do not execute.

Another important point to note is that the 'if' condition is also not enclosed inside braces like other programming languages. The 'if' block starts with a colon, followed by statements indented to the right.

It is pertinent to mention here that all the statements within a code block should have same indentation or else Python will throw an error. Take a look at the following example.

```
if 10 > 3:
    print("This is inside if block")
        print("This has different indentation")

print("This is outside if block")
```

If you try to run the above script, you will get an error that looks like this:

```
File "<ipython-input-4-288993e82763>", line 3
  print("This has different indentation")
    ^
IndentationError: unexpected indent
```

There are several advantages of using indentation for code blocks rather than braces. Indentation forces developers to write readable code with fewer inconsistencies.

Python Identifiers

An Identifier in programming is a name assigned to any variable, function, module or a class. A Python identifier can contains letters from A-Z a-z, numbers from 0-9 and underscore. A python identifier name must begin with a letter or an underscore. Python is a case sensitive language which means "Customer" and "customer" are considered two different identifiers in Python.

Naming Conventions

Here are some python naming conventions:

- Package and module names are all lower case
- Classes are declared in bumpy case with first letter of the individual words capitalized. For instance "CustomerProductRecord" is a valid class name.

- For methods and functions convention is to use lowercase letters with individual words separated by underscores. For example person_name, get_age etc.
- Private variable names begin with single underscore
- Strongly private variable names begin with double underscore

Python Keywords

Keywords are special words that are reserved by python to perform special tasks. For example keyword class is used to define a class. Similarly keyword "for" is used to define a loop. ***Keywords cannot be used as identifier or constant names.*** Python has following set of keywords.

and	exec	not
assert	finally	or
break	For	Pass
class	From	Print

continue	global	Raise
def	If	Return
del	import	Try
elif	In	While
else	Is	With
except	lambda	Yield

Capturing User Input

Capturing user input is one of the most fundamental programming tasks. Python makes it simple. In Python 3, you can use the input() function and pass it the string that you want to display to the user. Take a look at the following screen shot:

```
text = input("Please enter your name!")
Please enter your name!
```

Anything you enter in the textbox will be stored inside the text variable.

What's next?

This chapter presented brief overview of Python syntax. The rest of the book follows the conventions and syntax described in this chapter. In the next chapter, we will study basic Python data types. We shall see what different types of data python can hold and how to declare variables to store the data. Happy Coding!!!

Chapter 4

Variables and Data Types

A software application consists of two fundamental parts: Logic and Data. Logic consists of the functionalities that are applied on data to accomplish a particular task. Application data can be stored in memory or hard disk. Files and databases are used to store data on hard disk. In memory, data is stored in the form of variables.

Definition of Variable

Variable in programming is a memory location used to store some value. Whenever you store a value in a variable, that value is actually being stored at physical location in memory. Variables can be thought of as reference to physical memory location. The size of the memory reserved for a variable depends upon the type of value stored in the variable.

Creating a Variable

It is very easy to create a variable in Python. The assignment operator "=" is used for this purpose. The value to the left of the assignment operator is the variable identifier or name of the variable. The value to the right of the operator is the value assigned to the variable. Take a look at the following code snippet.

```
Name  = 'Mike'        # A string
variable
Age   = 15            # An integer
variable
Score = 102.5         # A floating
type variable
Pass  = True          # A boolean
Variable
```

In the script above we created four different types of variables. You can see that we did not specify the type of variable with the variable name. For instance we did not write "string Name" or "int Age". We only wrote the variable name. This is because Python is a loosely typed language. Depending upon the value being stored in a variable, Python assigns type to the variable at runtime. For instance when Python interpreter interprets the line "Age = 15", it checks the type of the value which is integer in this case. Hence, Python understands that Age is an integer type variable.

To check type of a variable, pass the variable name to "type" function as shown below:

```
type(Age)
```

You will see that the above script, when run, prints "int" in the output which is basically the type of Age variable.

Python allows multiple assignment which means that you can assign one value to multiple variables at the same time. Take a look at the following script:

```
Age = Number = Point = 20
#Multiple Assignment

print (Age)
print (Number)
print (Point)
```

In the script above, integer 20 is assigned to three variables: Age, Number and Point. If you print the value of these three variables, you will see 20 thrice in the output.

Python Data Types

A programming application needs to store variety of data. Consider scenario of a banking application that needs to store customer information. For instance, a person's name and mobile number; whether he is a defaulter or not; collection of items that he/she has loaned and so on. To store such variety of information, different data types are required. While you can create custom data types in the form of classes, Python provides six standard data types out of the box. They are:

- Strings
- Numbers
- Booleans
- Lists
- Tuples
- Dictionaries

Strings

Python treats string as sequence of characters. To create strings in Python, you can use single as well as double quotes. Take a look at the following script:

```
first_name = 'mike' # String
with single quotation
last_name = " johns" # String
with double quotation
full_name  =  first_name  +
last_name      #      string
concatenation using +
print(full_name)
```

In the above script we created three string variables: first_name, last_name and full_name. String with single quotes is used to initialize the variable "first_name" while string with double quotes initializes the variable "last_name". The variable full_name contains the concatenation of the first_name and last_name variables. Running the above script returns following output:

```
mike johns
```

Numbers

There are four types of numeric data in python:

- int (Stores integer e.g 10)
- float (Stores floating point numbers e.g 2.5)
- long (Stores long integer such as 48646684333)
- complex (Complex number such as 7j+4847k)

To create a numeric Python variable, simply assign a number to variable. In the following script we create four different types of numeric objects and print them on the console.

```
int_num = 10          # integer
float_num = 156.2   #float
long_num = -0.5977485613454646
#long
complex_num      =      -.785+7J
#Complex
```

```
print(int_num)
print(float_num)
print(long_num)
print(complex_num)
```

The output of the above script will be as follows:

```
10
156.2
-0.5977485613454646
(-0.785+7j)
```

Boolean

Boolean variables are used to store Boolean values. True and False are the two Boolean values in Python. Take a look at the following example:

```
defaulter = True
has_car = False

print(defaulter and has_car)
```

In the script above we created two Boolean variables "defaulter" and "has_car" with values True and False respectively. We then print the result of the AND operation on both of these variables. Since the AND operation between True and False returns false, you will see false in the output. We will study more about the logical operators in the next chapter.

Lists

In Python, List data type is used to store collection of values. Lists are similar to arrays in any other programming language. However Python lists can store values of different types. To create a list opening and closing square brackets are used. Each item in the list is separated from the other with a comma. Take a look at the following example.

```
cars = ['Honda', 'Toyota',
'Audi', 'Ford', 'Suzuki',
'Mercedez']
print(len(cars))  #finds total
items in string
```

```
print(cars)
```

In the script above we created a list named cars. The list contains six string values i.e. car names. Next we printed the size of the list using len function. Finally we print the list on console.

The output looks like this:

```
6
['Honda', 'Toyota', 'Audi', 'Ford', 'Suzuki', 'Mercedez']
```

Tuples

Tuples are similar to lists with two major differences. Firstly, opening and closing braces are used to create tuples instead of lists that use square brackets. Secondly, tuple once created is immutable which means that you cannot change tuple values once it is created. The following example clarifies this concept.

```
cars = ['Honda', 'Toyota',
'Audi', 'Ford', 'Suzuki',
'Mercedez']
```

```
cars2   =     ('Honda',  'Toyota',
'Audi',    'Ford',    'Suzuki',
'Mercedez')


cars [3] = 'WV'


cars2 [3] = 'WV'
```

In the above script we created a list named cars and a tuple named cars2. Both the list and tuple contains list of car names. We then try to update the third index of the list as well as tuple with a new value. The list will be updated but an error will be thrown while trying to update the tuple's third index. This is due to the fact that tuple, once created cannot be modified with new values. The error looks like this:

```
----------------------------------------------------------------
TypeError                              Traceback (most recent call last)
<ipython-input-17-d571617c1fe4> in <module>()
      5 cars [3] = 'WV'
      6
----> 7 cars2 [3] = 'WV'

TypeError: 'tuple' object does not support item assignment
```

Dictionaries

Dictionaries store collection of data in the form of key-value pairs. Each key-value pair is separated from the other via comma. Keys and values are separated from each other via colon. Dictionary items can be accessed via index as well as keys. To create dictionaries you need to add key-value pairs inside opening and closing parenthesis. Take a look at the following example.

```
cars      =      {'Name':'Audi',
'Model':           2008,
'Color':'Black'}


print(cars['Color'])
print(cars.keys())
print(cars.values())
```

In the above script we created a dictionary named cars. The dictionary contains three key-value pairs i.e. 3 items. To access value, we can pass key to the brackets that follow dictionary name. Similarly we can use keys() and values() methods to retrieve all the keys and values from a dictionary, respectively. The output of the script above looks like this:

```
Black
dict_keys(['Name', 'Model', 'Color'])
dict_values(['Audi', 2008, 'Black'])
```

What's next?

This chapter briefly sheds light on variables and data types in Python. In the next chapter we will start our discussion about Python operators. Happy Coding!

Chapter 5

Operators

Operators in programming are literals used to perform specific logical, relational or mathematical operations on the operands. Python operators can be divided into following five categories:

- Arithmetic

- Logical

- Comparison

- Assignment

- Membership operators

In this chapter we will discuss these operators with the help of examples.

Arithmetic Operators

Arithmetic operators, as the name suggests, are used to perform arithmetic operations on the operands.

Suppose N1 = 10 and N2 = 5; take a look at the following table to understand arithmetic operators.

Operator Name	Symbol	Functionality	Example
Addition	+	Adds the operands on either side	N1 + N2 = 15
Subtraction	-	Subtracts the operands on either side	N1 − N2 = 5
Multiplication	*	Multiplies the operands on either side	N1 * N2 = 50

Division	/	Divides the operand on left by the one on right	N1 / N2 = 2
Modulus	%	Divides the operand on left by the one on right and returns remainder	N1 / N2 = 0
Exponent	**	Takes exponent of the operand on the left to the power of right	N1 ** N2 = 100000

Take a look at the following example to see arithmetic operators in action:

```
N1 = 10
N2 = 5

print(N1 + N2)
print(N1 - N2)
print(N1 * N2)
print(N1 / N2)
print(N1 ** N2)
```

The output of the script above looks like this:

```
15
5
50
2.0
100000
```

Logical Operators

Logical operators are used to perform logical functions such as AND, OR and NOT on the operands. The following table contains Python logical operators along with their description and functionality. Suppose N1 is True and N2 is false.

Operator	Symbol	Functionality	Example
Logical AND	and	If both the operands are true then condition becomes true.	(N1 and N2) = False
Logical OR	or	If any of the two operands are true then condition becomes true.	(N1 or N2) = True

Logical NOT	not	Used to reverse the logical state of its operand.	not(N1 and N2) =True

Take a look at the following example to see logical operators in action:

```
N1 = True
N2 = False

print(N1 and N2)
print(N1 or N2)
print(not(N1 and N2))
```

The output of the above script looks like this:

```
False
True
True
```

Comparison Operators

Comparison operators are used to compare the values contained by the operands and returns true or false depending upon the relationship between the operands. Comparison operators are also commonly known as relational operators. Suppose N1 is equal to 10 and N2 is equal to 5, take a look a look at the following table to understand comparison operators.

Operator	Symbol	Description	Example
Equality	==	Returns true if values of both the operands are equal	(N1 == N2) = false
Inequality	!=	Returns true if values of both the operands are not equal	(N1 != N2) = true
Greater than	>	Returns true if value of the left operand is greater than the right one	(N1 > N2) = true
Smaller than	<	Returns true if value of the left operand is smaller than the right one	(N1 < N2) = false

Greater than or equal to	>=	Returns true if value of the left operand is greater than or equal to the right one	(N1 >=N2) = true
Smaller than or equal to	<=	Returns true if value of the left operand is smaller than or equal to the right one	(N1 <= N2) = false

Take a look at the following example to see comparison operators in action:

```
N1 = 10
N2 = 5

print(N1 == N2)
print(N1 != N2)
print(N1 > N2)
print(N1 < N2)
print(N1 >= N2)
print(N1 <= N2)
```

The output of the script above looks like this:

```
False
True
True
False
True
False
```

Assignment Operators

Assignment operators are used to assign values to the operand. The table below contains information about Python assignment operators. Suppose N1 is equal to 10 and N2 is equal to 5.

Operator	Symbol	Description	Example
Assignment	=	Used to assign value of the right operand to the right.	R = N1 + N2 assigns 15 to R
Add and assign	+=	Adds the operands on either side and assigns the result to the left operand	N1 += N2 assigns 15 to N1
Subtract and assign	-=	Subtracts the operands on either side and assigns the	N1 -= N2 assigns 5 to N1

		result to the left operand	
Multiply and Assign	*=	Multiplies the operands on either side and assigns the result to the left operand	N1 *= N2 assigns 50 to N1
Divide and Assign	/=	Divides the operands on the left by the right and assigns the result to the left operand	N1 *= N2 assigns 2 to N1
Take modulus and assign	%=	Divides the operands on the left by the right and assigns the remainder to the left operand	N1 %= N2 assigns 0 to N1
Take exponent and assign	**=	Takes exponent of the operand on the left to the power of right and assign the remainder to the left operand	N1 **= N2 assigns 100000 to N1

Take a look at the following example to see assignment operators in action:

```
N1 = 10; N2 = 5
```

```
R = N1 + N2
print(R)


N1 = 10; N2 = 5
N1 += N2
print(N1)


N1 = 10; N2 = 5
N1 -= N2
print(N1)


N1 = 10; N2 = 5
N1 *= N2
print(N1)


N1 = 10; N2 = 5
N1 /= N2
print(N1)


N1 = 10; N2 = 5
N1 %= N2
```

```
print(N1)


N1 = 10; N2 = 5
N1 **= N2
print(N1)
```

The output of the script above looks like this:

```
15
15
5
50
2.0
0
100000
```

Membership Operators

Membership operators are used to check whether the value stored in the operand exists in a particular sequence or not. There are two types of membership operators in Python: 'in' and 'not in'. The in operator returns true if a value is found in a particular sequence. The "not in" operator returns true in the reverse case. Take a look at the following example to see membership operators in action.

```
cars = ['Honda', 'Toyota', 'Audi', 'Ford', 'Camery']
print('Honda' in cars)    # Returns True
print('BMW' in cars) # Returns False
print('Honda' not in cars)    # Returns False
print('BMW' not in cars)    # Returns True
```

The script above returns following output:

```
True
False
False
True
```

What's Next?

In this chapter, we studied basic Python operators with the help of different examples. In the next chapter we will start our discussion about conditional statements. We will study what different types of conditional statements are supported by Python and how they work. Happy Coding!!!

Chapter 6

Conditional Statements

Conditional statements in programming are used to control the flow of a program. Take example of the login page of a website. It asks user to enter username and password. If the username and password are valid, user is granted access to his personal account, otherwise a message is displayed informing the user that username or password is not correct. Here behind the scene conditional statements are being used to check if the password is correct and depending the validation of password, user is either granted access to his personal account or prompted to enter his username and password again. In short, conditional statements are controlling the flow of the application.

There are three main types of conditional statements in Python:

- If
- else
- elif

The "if" statement

The "if" statement is used to evaluate a block of code if the expression that follows it, evaluates to true. This statement may sound complex at the moment but will make sense once you see working example of the "if" statement. Take a look:

```
num1 = 10
num2 = 20


if num2 > num1:
    print("num2   is   greater
than num1")
```

In the script above we create two variables num1 and num2 with values 10 and 20 respectively. Next, we write an "if" statement that evaluates if num2 is greater than num1, which returns true. Hence the statement that prints "num1 is greater than num2" executes. The output looks like this:

```
num2 is greater than num1
```

Now let's evaluate if num2 is smaller than num1. Execute the following script:

```
num1 = 10
num2 = 20
```

```
if num2 < num1:

    print("num2    is    smaller
than num1")
```

Since num2 is not smaller than num1, therefore the "if" block will not execute and you will see nothing in the output.

Conjugating two or more conditions

You can also conjugate two or more than two expressions using logical "OR" and "AND" operators. Take a look at the following script:

```
num1 = 10
num2 = 20
num3 = 30


if num2 < num1 or num3 > num2
:

    print("num2    is    smaller
than num1 OR num3 is greater
than num2")
```

In the script above, two conditions are evaluated conjugated using logical OR operator. The first condition checks if num2 is greater than num1, which is not true. The second condition evaluates if num3 is greater than num2, which returns true. Since the conditions are conjugated using an OR operator, the overall result will be true, hence the statements in the "if" block will execute. The output of the script above looks like this:

```
num2 is smaller than num1 OR num3 is greater than num2
```

Nested "if" statements

You can nest "if" statement inside other "if" statements. Take a look at the following example:

```
num1 = 10
num2 = 20
num3 = 30


if num2 > num1:
```

```
if num3 > num2:

        print("num2 is greater
than num1 and num3 is greater
than num2")
```

The output will look like this:

```
num2 is smaller than num1 OR num3 is greater than num2
```

The "else" statement

The "if" block executes only if the condition that follows it, returns true. What if we want to execute an alternate set of statements if the condition returns false? The "else" statement performs exactly this task. Take a look at the following statement:

```
num1 = 10
num2 = 20


if num1 > num2:

    print("num1    is    greater
than num2")

else:

    print("num2    is    greater
than num1")
```

In the script above the "if" condition checks if num1 is greater than num2, which evaluates to false. Hence, the "if" block is not executed. The control shifts to "else" statement and the statement in the else block executes. The output of the script above looks like this:

```
num2 is greater than num1
```

The "elif" statement

You can evaluate multiple conditions using the "elif" statement. This is best explained with the help of an example:

```
num1 = 10
num2 = 20
num3 = 30
```

```
if num1 > num2:
    print("num1    is    greater
than num2")
elif num2 > num3:
    print("num2    is    greater
than num3")
elif num3 > num2:
    print("num3    is    greater
than num1")
else:
    print("None    of    the
conditions are true")
```

In the script above, the "if" statement checks if num1 is greater than num2, which evaluates to false. Hence the control shifts to first "elif" statement. The first "elif" statement checks if num2 is greater than num3, which again evaluates to false. Hence the control shifts to the next "elif" statement which evaluates to true since num3 is actually greater than num2. Hence the code block for the second "elif" statement will be executed. The output of the script above looks like this:

```
num3 is greater than num1
```

If the conditions for the "if" and all the "elif" statements evaluate to false, the code block that follows the else statement executes.

Nested "elif" Statements

Like "if" statement, you can also have nested "elif" statements. Take a look at the following example.

```
num1 = 10
num2 = 20
num3 = 30


if num1 > num2:
    print("num1   is   greater
than num2")
elif num2 > num3:
    print("num2   is   greater
than num3")
elif num3 > num2:
```

```python
    if num1 > num3:
        print("num1 is greater than num3")
    elif num2 > num1:
        print("num2 is greater than num1 but smaller than num3")
else:
    print("None of the conditions are true")
```

In the script above, from the first level, the second "elif" statement that checks if num3 is greater than num2 evaluates to true. However, inside this "elif" statement there are further nested "if" and "elif" statements. The inner "if" statement checks if num1 is greater than num3 which returns false. The control shifts to the inner "elif" statement which checks if num2 is greater than num1, which evaluates to true. Hence, the statement followed by the inner "elif" block executes. The output of the above script looks like this:

```
num2 is greater than num1 but smaller than num3
```

What's Next?

In this chapter, we studied different types of conditional statements and how they can be used to control the flow of a program. In the next chapter we will start our discussion about iteration statements. We will see different types of iteration statements along with their usage. Happy Coding!!!

Chapter 7

Iteration Statements (Loops)

Iteration statements are used to repeatedly execute a piece of code for specific number of times or until a certain condition is satisfied. Imagine you have to perform a task as simple as printing a five character string on screen, 100 times. You will have to write 100 lines of code. Or you will have to use copy-paste. Consider a scenario where you have to repeatedly execute a huge chunk of code. In such a case, it is not convenient to copy paste the code for several reasons:

firstly it will significantly increase the code size and secondly it will be difficult to maintain such a code leading to errors. Luckily, iteration statements come to our rescue in such scenarios. Iteration statements are also commonly known as loops.

There are two types of iteration statements in Python:

- The "for" loop
- The "while" loop

The "for" loop

The "for" loop is used to iterate over a collection of items e.g. list, tuple, dictionary etc. The syntax of for loop is as follows:

```
for i in [list]:
    statement 1 …
    statement 2 …
```

Here 'i' is any variable to which a value can be assigned. List is the list of the elements that the "for" loop iterates upon. Take a look

at the following example to see for loop in
action:

```
cars                                    =
['Audi','BMW','Toyota','Honda'
,'Ford']
for car in cars:
    print(car)
```

In the script above we create a list of car
names. We then use "for" loop to iterate
over this list. Let's understand how for loop
actually executes behind the scene. During
the first iteration the first item of the cars list
(the item at index 0) which is "Audi" in this
case, is assigned to the car variable. The
value of the car variable is printed on the
screen. During the second iteration, the
second list items is stored in the car variable
and printed on the screen and so on. The
output of the script above looks like this:

```
Audi
BMW
Toyota
Honda
Ford
```

Using Range Function

What if we want to execute a particular statement without having a list? We can use "range" function to do so. Basically range function also returns an iterate-able sequence that the "for" loop can iterate on. For instance if we want to execute a "for" loop 10 times, we can use range function as follows. Take a look at the following example:

```
for i in range(10):
    print(i)
```

The range function returns a sequence with specified number of integers, starting from 0. The output of the above script will be integers from 0 to 9.

Range function can also be used create a sequence of integers between a specific range. For instance if you want to create sequence of integers from 50 to 100, you can do so as follows:

```
for i in range(50,101):
    print(i)
```

Remember that the sequence returned by range function contains the integer including the lower bound but not the upper bound. Therefore the above script will return integer from 50 to 100 but not 101.

Iterating Over a String

For loop can also be used to iterate over a string. This is because string is actually sequence of characters. Have a look at the script below:

```
for c in 'Hello world':
    print(c)
```

The output will look like this:

```
H
e
l
l
o

w
o
r
l
d
```

The "while" loop

Number of times a "for" loop executes is equal to the number of items in the sequence that the loop operates upon. What if we want a loop that terminates when certain condition is satisfied? The "while" loop is the answer; The "while" loop executes, until a certain condition is met. Syntax of "while" loop is as follows:

```
while (expression = true):
    statement1 …
```

```
    statement2 ...
```

Basically "while" loop checks whether the expression that follows it, evaluates to true or not. It keeps executing until the expression returns true.

Take a look at the following script to understand "while" loop

```
i = 1
while i < 11:
    print(i)
    i = i+1
```

In the script above we initialize a variable "i" with integer 1. We then create a "while" loop which checks if the value of variable "i" is less than 11. With each iteration, inside the "while" loop we increment the value of "i" by 1. After the loop has executed 10 times, the value of "i" becomes 11. Therefore, the condition "i" is less than 11 returns false, hence "while" loop terminates.

Let's try to print table of 9 using "while" loop. Take a look at the following script:

```
i = 1
while i < 11:
    print('9 x '+ str(i) + ' =
' + str(i * 9))
    i = i+1
```

The output of the script above looks like this:

```
9 x 1 = 9
9 x 2 = 18
9 x 3 = 27
9 x 4 = 36
9 x 5 = 45
9 x 6 = 54
9 x 7 = 63
9 x 8 = 72
9 x 9 = 81
9 x 10 = 90
```

Continue Statement

Continue statement is used to skip the remaining statements in the loop and to shift the control back to the beginning of the loop. Continue statement can be used inside "for" as well as "while" loop.

Take a look at the following example to see continue statement in action.

```
for i in range(1,11):
    if(i%2) != 0:
        continue
    print(i)
```

In the script above we use "for" loop that iterates over sequence of integers from 1 to 10. In each iteration, we check if the integer is even. To do so, we divide the integer by 2 and check if the result is 0. If the integer is even we do print it on the console, else if the integer is not even, we use continue statement to go back to the beginning of the for loop body, skipping the print statement. The output of the script contains even numbers between 2 and 10 as shown below:

```
2
4
6
8
10
```

Break Statement

Break statement is used to terminate the execution of a loop. Break statement can be used inside "for" as well as "while" loops. Take a look at the following statement to see break statement in action.

```
for i in range(1,11):
    if(i > 5):
        break
    print(i)
```

In the script above, the "for" loop is terminated using break statement when the value of "i" becomes greater than 5.

What's Next?

We have covered most of the fundamental Python concepts. From the next chapter onwards we will divert our attention towards in-depth analysis of advanced Python concepts. In the next chapter we will study Python sequences in detail. We will have an in-depth analysis of lists, tuples and dictionaries and the functions that can be performed on these sequences. Happy Coding!!!

Chapter 8

Lists, Tuples and Dictionaries

We briefly reviewed lists, tuples and dictionaries in *Chapter 4: Variables and Data Types*. They are some of the most important data structures in Python. In this chapter we will see lists, tuples and dictionaries in detail. We will see how they work what are some of the different types of functions associated with them.

Lists

A list in Python is similar to an array in other programming languages. A list stores collection of objects of different types and is mutable.

Creating a List

There are different ways to create a list. The simplest way to create a list is by enclosing comma separated list of items within square brackets and assigning it to a variable as shown in the example below:

```
colors = ['Red', 'Green', 'Blue', 'Yellow', 'White']
```

The script above creates a list named colors. Other ways to create a list are by using constructors [] and list(). As shown below.

```
colors2 = []
colors3 = list()
```

The above script creates two empty lists: colors2 and colors3.

To create list of sequence of integers you can use *range* function and convert into list using list function. The range function returns a list of sequence of integers from 0 to 1 less than the value passed to it as parameter as shown below:

```
nums = list(range(10))
nums
```

The list nums contains integers from 0 to 9. To create a list of sequence of integers between a specified range, you can pass two values to range function. The first value specifies the lower bound (included in the resultant sequence) and the second value specifies the upper bound (excluded in the resultant sequence). The following range function returns list of integers from 50 to 100.

```
nums = list(range(50,101))
nums
```

Accessing List Elements

Lists are indexed which means you can use indexes to access list elements. Lists follow zero based indexes. The first element is stored at the 0th index while the last element is stored at K-1 index, where K is the total number of elements in the list.

In the following example we will access the 2nd element of the list colors:

```
colors = ['Red', 'Green', 'Blue', 'Yellow', 'White']
print(colors[1])
```

The above script prints 'Green' to the output console.

Lists are mutable, which means that you can change item value stored at a particular index. Let's change the value stored at third index from 'Blue' to 'Black'.

```
colors = ['Red', 'Green', 'Blue', 'Yellow', 'White']
print(colors)
colors[2] = 'Black'
print(colors)
```

In the script above we print the colors list on the screen before and after setting the value of the item at third index to 'Black'. The output looks like this:

```
['Red', 'Green', 'Blue', 'Yellow', 'White']
['Red', 'Green', 'Black', 'Yellow', 'White']
```

You can also access multiple list elements at one time using slice operator i.e. colon (:). For instance if you want to access the first three elements of a list, you can use slice operator as follows:

```
colors = ['Red', 'Green', 'Blue', 'Yellow', 'White']
sublist = colors[:3]
print(sublist)
```

The above script returns following result:

```
['Red', 'Green', 'Blue']
```

Similarly, if you want to access the last three elements of a list, execute the following script:

```
colors = ['Red', 'Green', 'Blue', 'Yellow', 'White']
sublist = colors[-3:]
print(sublist)
```

The result looks like this:

```
['Blue', 'Yellow', 'White']
```

Finally, you can also access range of items from a list using slice operator.

```
colors = ['Red', 'Green', 'Blue', 'Yellow', 'White']
sublist = colors[2:4]
print(sublist)
```

The above function returns range of elements from the 2nd index up to one less than the 4th index i.e. elements at index 2 and 3. The output looks like this:

```
['Blue', 'Yellow']
```

Appending elements to a list

The *append* function can be used to append elements to a list. The item to append is passed as parameter to the 'append' function. Take a look at the following example:

```
colors = ['Red', 'Green', 'Blue', 'Yellow', 'White']
print(colors)
colors.append('Orange')
```

```
print(colors)
```

In the script above, we create a list, colors with five items. We print the list on console. We then append an item to the list and again print the list on the console. The output looks like this:

```
['Red', 'Green', 'Blue', 'Yellow', 'White']
['Red', 'Green', 'Blue', 'Yellow', 'White', 'Orange']
```

You can see the newly appended item 'Orange' in the output.

Removing Element from a List

The *remove* function is used to remove element from a list. The element to remove is passed as parameter to the method.

```
colors = ['Red', 'Green', 'Blue', 'Yellow', 'White']
print(colors)
colors.remove('Blue')
print(colors)
```

The output of the script above looks like this:

```
['Red', 'Green', 'Blue', 'Yellow', 'White']
['Red', 'Green', 'Yellow', 'White']
```

You can see that the item 'Blue' has been removed from the list. List elements can also be deleted using index numbers.

```
colors = ['Red', 'Green',
'Blue', 'Yellow', 'White']
print(colors)
del colors[2]
print(colors)
```

To delete list element by index you have to use *del* function followed by the name of the list and the index value passed inside square brackets.

Concatenating List

You can concatenate one list with the other using *'+'* symbol as shown below:

```
nums1 = [2, 4, 6, 8, 10]
nums2 = [1, 3, 5, 7, 9]

result = nums1 + nums2
```

```
print(result)
```

The output looks like this:

```
[2, 4, 6, 8, 10, 1, 3, 5, 7, 9]
```

You can see that the second list is concatenated at the end of the first list.

Using in and not in Functions with Lists

The 'in' and 'not in' functions can be used to check whether an element exists in a string or not.

```
colors = ['Red', 'Green',
'Blue', 'Yellow', 'White']
print('Green' in colors)
print('Orange' in colors)
print('Black' not in colors)
print('Blue' not in colors)
```

The in function returns true for 'Green in colors' since the item 'Green' actually exists within the color string. Similarly for 'Blue' not in colors, false will be returned since

'Blue' exists in colors list. The output for the script above looks like this:

```
True
False
True
False
```

Finding length of List

The *len* function can be used to find total number of elements in a list.

```
colors = ['Red', 'Green',
'Blue', 'Yellow', 'White']
print(len(colors))
```

The script above returns 5, since there are five elements in the colors list.

Sorting a List

You can sort and reverse elements of a list. The elements are sorted alphabetically in case of strings and in ascending order in case of numeric values. Take a look at the following example:

```
colors  =  ['Red',  'Green',
'Blue', 'Yellow', 'White']
colors.sort()
print(colors)

nums = [12, 4, 66, 35, 7]
nums.sort()
print(nums)
```

To sort the list, **sort** function is called on the list. Remember, sorting is in-place which means that the existing list is changed rather than returning a new list. The output of the script above looks like this:

```
['Blue', 'Green', 'Red', 'White', 'Yellow']
[4, 7, 12, 35, 66]
```

List of Lists (Matrices)

Lists can be nested inside another list, resulting in a matrix. In the following example we nest three lists with four items inside another list resulting in '3 x 4' matrix.

```
colors = [[1,15,20,36],
          [41,20,54,47],
```

```
                [74,45,69,47]]
```

List of lists or matrices also follow zero based index. To access first list, you need to pass zero as index to the outer list. Take a look at the following example:

```
colors = [[1,15,20,36],
          [41,20,54,47],
          [74,45,69,47]]
print(colors[0])
```

The above script prints the first list inside the parent list as shown below:

```
[1, 15, 20, 36]
```

To access a particular value in nested list, first you have to specify the index for the nested list and then the index for the particular value inside that list. For instance if you want to access the element at the third index belonging to the list at first index i.e. 47, you can use the following syntax.

```
colors = [[1,15,20,36],
          [41,20,54,47],
```

```
            [74,45,69,47]]
print(type(colors))
num = colors[1][3]
print(num)
```

Tuples

Like lists, tuples are also used to store collection of different types of objects. However, unlike lists, tuples are immutable which means that once created, tuple elements cannot be changed. You cannot update a tuple, cannot delete tuple element and cannot add new elements to a tuple.

Creating a Tuple

To create a tuple, assign a comma separated list of objects, enclosed within a parenthesis to a variable. Take a look at the following script:

```
colors   =   ('Red',   'Green',
'Blue', 'Yellow', 'White')
type(colors)
```

In the script above we create a tuple named colors with five items. To confirm the type of the colors variable we use *type* function which confirms that the type of the variable colors is actually a tuple.

Accessing Tuple Elements

Tuple elements can be accessed just like lists using indexes. Take a look at the following script:

```
colors = ('Red', 'Green',
'Blue', 'Yellow', 'White')
print(colors[2])
```

The script above prints tuple element at second index which is 'Blue'.

The slice operator works for tuples too. Take a look at the following example:

```
colors = ('Red', 'Green',
'Blue', 'Yellow', 'White')
print(colors[:3]) # Accessing
first three elements
```

```
colors = ('Red', 'Green',
'Blue', 'Yellow', 'White')
print(colors[-3:]) # Accessing
last three elements
```

```
colors = ('Red', 'Green',
'Blue', 'Yellow', 'White')
print(colors[1:3]) # Accessing
elements at index 1 and 2
```

The output of the script above looks like this:

```
('Red', 'Green', 'Blue')
('Blue', 'Yellow', 'White')
('Green', 'Blue')
```

Updating a Tuple

We know that tuples are immutable. The elements in a tuple cannot be updated, added or removed. Let's try to modify the tuple element and verify this fact.

```
colors = ('Red', 'Green',
'Blue', 'Yellow', 'White')
colors[2] = 'Orange'
```

In the script above, we assign a new value to the 2nd index of the colors tuple. Try to execute the script above. The following error will occur:

```
---------------------------------------------------------------------------
TypeError                                 Traceback (most recent call last)
<ipython-input-7-826025ebd4a8> in <module>()
      1 colors = ('Red', 'Green', 'Blue', 'Yellow', 'White')
----> 2 colors[2] = 'Orange'

TypeError: 'tuple' object does not support item assignment
```

The error clearly says that the new elements cannot be assigned to a tuple.

Finding length of a Tuple

Tuple length can be found using *len* function. This is similar to list. Take a look at the following script:

```
colors = ('Red', 'Green', 'Blue', 'Yellow', 'White')
print(len(colors))
```

The script above returns 5 i.e. total number of elements in the colors tuple.

Finding an Element in Tuple with 'in' and 'not in' Functions

The 'in' and 'not in' functions can be used with tuples to find if an element exists within the tuple. Take a look at the following script:

```
colors = ('Red', 'Green',
'Blue', 'Yellow', 'White')
print('Green' in colors)
print('Orange' in colors)
print('Black' not in colors)
print('Blue' not in colors)
```

The output of the script above looks like this:

```
True
False
True
False
```

Tuple Concatenation

Like lists, the addition operator '+' can be used to concatenate two tuples. In fact, this is one of the ways to add an element to a tuple.

```
colors = ('Red', 'Green',
'Blue', 'Yellow', 'White')
orange_color = ('Orange',)
```

```
newcolors       =       colors       +
orange_color
print(newcolors)
```

In the script above, we create a tuple colors with five elements. We then create another tuple namely orange_color with one string element 'Orange'. Both the tuples are concatenated which returns a new tuple with 6 elements. The resultant tuple is then printed to the output console. This is one of the ways to add a new element to an existing tuple. The output of the script above looks like this:

```
('Red', 'Green', 'Blue', 'Yellow', 'White', 'Orange')
```

Finding Maximum and Minimum Element within a Tuple

The max and min functions are used to find the maximum and minimum values within a tuple. Take a look at the following script:

```
nums = (2, 4, 6, 8, 10)
print(min(nums))      #      prints
maximum value in tuple
```

```
print(max(nums))    #    prints
minimum value in tuple
```

The output of the script above looks like this:

```
2
10
```

The min and max functions can also be used with a List.

Converting List to Tuples

You can convert a list into tuple by passing list to the constructor of the tuple. Take a look at the following example:

```
colors   =   ['Red',   'Green',
'Blue', 'Yellow', 'White']
print(type(colors))
colors_tuple = tuple(colors)
print(colors_tuple)
```

In the script above we create a list named colors with 5 items. We then check the type of the colors variable. We then create another variable colors_tuple. The colors list is passed to the constructor of the tuple and the resultant tuple is stored in the colors_tuple variable. The newly created colors_tuple is then printed on the console. The output of the script above looks like this:

```
<class 'list'>
('Red', 'Green', 'Blue', 'Yellow', 'White')
```

Dictionaries

Dictionaries store collection of items in the form of key-value pairs. Keys and values are for each item is separated with a colon ':'. Each element is separated from the other by a comma. The comma separated list of items is enclosed by braces. Dictionaries are mutable, which means that you can update or delete an item from a dictionary and can also add new items to a dictionary.

Creating a Dictionary

```
cars       =       {'name':'Honda',
'model':2013,
'color':'Yellow', 'Air bags':
True}
type(cars)
```

In the script above, we create dictionary cars with 4 items. We then used type function to confirm the type of the cars variable which returns 'dict'.

Accessing Dictionary items

Items within a dictionary can be accessed by passing key as index. Take a look at the following example.

```
cars     =     {'name':'Honda',
'model':2013,
'color':'Yellow',  'Air  bags':
True}
model = cars['model']
print(model)
```

In the script above the value for the item with key 'model' is being accessed by passing the key as index value. You will see 2013 in the output.

You can also access all the keys and values within a dictionary using *keys* and *values* function as shown below:

```
cars     =     {'name':'Honda',
'model':2013,
```

```
'color':'Yellow', 'Air bags':
True}

print(cars.keys()) # Accessing
keys from dictionary

print(cars.values())         #
Accessing    values    from
dictionary
```

The output of the script above looks like this:

```
dict_keys(['name', 'model', 'color', 'Air bags'])
dict_values(['Honda', 2013, 'Yellow', True])
```

You can also get items from a dictionary in the form of key-value pairs using *items* function. Take a look at the following example:

```
cars     =     {'name':'Honda',
'model':2013,
'color':'Yellow', 'Air bags':
True}

print(cars.items())          #
Accessing    items    from
dictionary
```

The output of the script above looks like this:

```
dict_items([('name', 'Honda'), ('model', 2013), ('color', 'Yellow'), ('Air bags', True)])
```

Iterating over Dictionary Items, Keys and Values

The 'items', 'keys' and 'values' functions return sequences that can be iterated using for loops. Take a look at the following example:

```
cars      =      {'name':'Honda',
'model':2013,
'color':'Yellow', 'Air bags':
True}
for item in cars.items():
    print(item)
```

The output of the script above looks like this:

```
('name', 'Honda')
('model', 2013)
('color', 'Yellow')
('Air bags', True)
```

Similarly, keys and values can also be iterated using for loops as shown in the following examples:

```
cars      =      {'name':'Honda',
'model':2013,
```

```
'color':'Yellow', 'Air bags':
True}
```

```
for key in cars.keys():
    print(key)
```

Output:

```
name
model
color
Air bags
```

Similarly for values:

```
cars        =        {'name':'Honda',
'model':2013,
'color':'Yellow', 'Air bags':
True}
```

```
for value in cars.values():
    print(value)
```

Output:

```
Honda
2013
Yellow
True
```

Adding Item to a dictionary

It is very easy to add a new item to a dictionary. You simply have to pass new key in index and assign it some value. Take a look at the following example:

```
cars      =      {'name':'Honda',
'model':2013,
'color':'Yellow', 'Air bags':
True}
print(cars)
cars['capacity'] = 500
print(cars)
```

In the script above, we create dictionary cars with four items. The dictionary is then printed on the console. Next, a new item is added to the dictionary. The dictionary is then printed on the console again. You will see that the new dictionary will contain five items. The output of the script above looks like this:

```
{'name': 'Honda', 'model': 2013, 'color': 'Yellow', 'Air bags': True}
{'name': 'Honda', 'model': 2013, 'color': 'Yellow', 'Air bags': True, 'capacity': 500}
```

Updating a Dictionary

To update dictionary, pass the key for which you want to update the value as index and assign it a new value. The following example makes it clearer:

```
cars        =      {'name':'Honda',
'model':2013,
'color':'Yellow', 'Air bags':
True}
print(cars)
cars['model'] = 2015
print(cars)
```

In the script above the items in the cars dictionary are printed before and after updating the value of the item with key 'model'. In the output you can see old and new value for 'model'. The output looks like this:

```
{'name': 'Honda', 'model': 2013, 'color': 'Yellow', 'Air bags': True}
{'name': 'Honda', 'model': 2015, 'color': 'Yellow', 'Air bags': True}
```

Deleting Dictionary Items

Like lists, the 'del' function can be used to delete items from a list. Have a look at the example below:

```
cars     =     {'name':'Honda',
'model':2013,
'color':'Yellow', 'Air bags':
True}
print(cars)
del cars['model']
print(cars)
```

To delete an item you use **del** function followed by the name of the dictionary. The key of the item that you want to delete is passed as index to the dictionary name. The script above shows items in the cards dictionary, before and after deleting the item with key 'model'. The output looks like this:

```
{'name': 'Honda', 'model': 2013, 'color': 'Yellow', 'Air bags': True}
{'name': 'Honda', 'color': 'Yellow', 'Air bags': True}
```

You can also delete all the items in a dictionary using **clear** function. The following example shows that:

```
cars        =        {'name':'Honda',
'model':2013,
'color':'Yellow',  'Air  bags':
True}

print(cars)

cars.clear()

print(cars)
```

The output of the script above looks like this:

```
{'name': 'Honda', 'model': 2013, 'color': 'Yellow', 'Air bags': True}
{}
```

Finding Dictionary Length

Like tuples and lists, length of a dictionary can be found using *len* function. Take a look at the following example:

```
cars        =        {'name':'Honda',
'model':2013,
'color':'Yellow',  'Air  bags':
True}
print(len(cars))
```

The script above returns 4 since there are 4 elements in the cars dictionary.

Checking the existence of an Item in Dictionary

To check if an item with certain key exists in a dictionary both *in* and **not in** methods can be used. Take a look at the following script:

```
cars      =      {'name':'Honda',
'model':2013,
'color':'Yellow', 'Air bags':
True}
print('color' in cars)
print('model' not in cars)
```

In the script above, the 'in' operator will return true since the key 'color' exists in the cars dictionary. However the operator 'not in' will return false since the key 'model' also exist in the cars dictionary. The output of the script above looks like this:

```
True
False
```

Copying Dictionaries

To copy one dictionary to the other, you can use *copy* function. Take a look at the following example:

```
cars       =       {'name':'Honda',
'model':2013,
'color':'Yellow', 'Air bags':
True}
cars2 = cars.copy()
print(cars2)
```

In the script above, we create dictionary cars with four items. We then copy this dictionary to another dictionary cars2. The newly created dictionary is then copied on the console. The output looks like this:

```
{'name': 'Honda', 'model': 2013, 'color': 'Yellow', 'Air bags': True}
```

What's next?

In this article we studied lists, tuples and dictionaries which are the most commonly used data structures for storing collections in Python. We saw how these collections are created and what are some of the most commonly used functions that can be applied to these collections. In the next chapter we will see different types of exceptions (errors) in python and how to handle these errors. Happy Coding!

Chapter 9

Exception Handling in Python

Errors and exceptions are part and parcel of a computer program in the development phase. The importance of handling exceptions is reflected by the fact that most of the software companies have a dedicated Quality Assurance (QA) department, responsible for ensuring that the final product is error free. In this chapter we will study what different types of python exceptions are, and how to handle these exceptions.

What is an Exception?

Exception is an event that disrupts the program execution. In simple words, when a Python scripts encounters a situation that it cannot deal with, it raises an exception. In Python, exception is raised in the form of object. Whenever an exception occurs, an object is initialized that contains information about the exception. An exception has to be handled in Python, otherwise the program quits executing.

Unlike most of the other programming languages, Python code is not evaluated at runtime since Python is a loosely typed language. The type of the variable is evaluated at runtime. There are both pros and cons of this approach. The major advantage of this approach is that a user doesn't have to specify the type of the variable while writing a code. A major drawback is that it can lead to exceptions at runtime. We will see this with the help of en example in this article, but first let's see how a simple exception is handled in Python

Syntax for Exception Handing

The syntax for exception handling is as follows:

```
Try:
     #the code that can raise
exception
except ExceptionA
```

```
        #the code to execute if
ExceptionA occurs
except ExceptionB
        #the code to execute if
ExceptionA occurs
except ExceptionC
        #the code to execute if
ExceptionA occurs
else:
        #Code to execute if there
is no exception
```

The code that you think can raise an exception is surrounded by *try* block followed by one or more *except* blocks depending upon the type of exceptions that you want to handle. If none of the exceptions occur, the *else* block executes.

Handling Single Exception

Example 1

Take a look at a very simple example of exception handling. Let us first write a program without exception handling. Execute the following script:

```
num1 = 10
num2 = 0
result = num1/num2
print(result)
```

In the script above we have two variables num1 and num2. We try to divide num1 by num2 and print the result on the console. However, num2 contains 0. Therefore, the division will not be successful since a number cannot be divided by zero. An error will be thrown that looks like this:

```
-----------------------------------------------------------------
ZeroDivisionError                    Traceback (most recent call last)
<ipython-input-14-0e801cc83d6e> in          ()
      1 num1 = 10
      2 num2 = 0
----> 3 result = num1/num2
      4 print(result)

ZeroDivisionError: division by zero
```

The name of the exception is "ZeroDivisionError" and it occurs when a number is divided by zero. Let's see how we can handle this exception.

Take a look at the following script:

```
try:
```

```
    num1 = 10
    num2 = 0
    result = num1/num2
    print(result)
except ZeroDivisionError:
    print ("Sorry, division by
zero not possible")
else:
    print("Program    executed
without an exception")
```

In the script above, the code that throws an exception is enclosed in a try block. In the previous example, the code threw ZeroDivisionError. Therefore, we handle this exception using **except** literal. Inside the *'except'* block the reason for the exception is printed. Finally, we have an else block that executes if the exception doesn't occur. Since we are dividing num1 by zero, the statement in the *'except'* block will execute and the output will look like this:

```
Sorry, divison by zero not possible
```

Now, if you change the value of num2 in code to 2. The exception will not occur and the output will display the code in the else block that looks like this:

```
5.0
Program executed without an exception
```

Hence, handling an exception prevents a program from crashing.

Example2

A program can throw multiple types of exceptions. Take a look at the following example to understand this concept:

```
try:
    result = a/b
    print(result)
except ZeroDivisionError:
    print ("Sorry, division by zero not possible")
else:
    print("Program    executed without an exception")
```

In the script above we try to divide 'a' by 'b'. We have handled the ZeroDivisonError exception. Therefore, if b contains 0, the exception will be handled. Else, if no exception occurs the *else* block will execute.

When you run the script above, you will see following exception:

```
--------------------------------------------------------------------
NameError                           Traceback (most recent call last)
<ipython-input-1-f57c54e1ec6b> in <module>()
      1 try:
----> 2     result = a/b
      3     print(result)
      4 except ZeroDivisionError:
      5     print ("Sorry, divison by zero not possible")

NameError: name 'a' is not defined
```

From the output you can see that the name of the exception is "NameError" and the exception says that the name 'a' is not defined. This means that we are using a variable without first defining it.

To handle this exception, execute the following code:

```
try:
    result = a/b
    print(result)
except NameError:
```

```python
    print ("Some variable/s are
not defined")
else:
    print("Program     executed
without an exception")
```

You can see that different types of exceptions are raised due to different reasons. In order to build a robust program, a user should handle all the possible exceptions. A list of different types of Python exceptions is available at the following link:

https://docs.python.org/3/library/exceptio
ns.html

Handling Multiple Exceptions

To handle multiple exceptions, you just have to stack one exception handling block over the other. Take a look at the following exception:

```python
try:
```

```
num1 = 10
num2 = 2
result = num1/num2
print(result)
except ZeroDivisionError:
    print ("Sorry, division by
zero not possible")
except NameError:
    print ("Some variable/s are
not defined")
else:
    print("Program    executed
without an exception")
```

In the script above, both the "ZeroDivisionError" and "NameError" exceptions are handled. Therefore, if you set the value of num2 to 0, the "ZeroDivisionError" exception will occur. However if you try to divide the num1 by 'b', the "NameError" exception will occur since the variable "b" is not defined. Finally if none of the exception occurs, the statement in the else block will execute.

Another way to handle multiple exceptions is by using Exception object which is base class for all the exceptions. The Exception object can be used to handle all types of exceptions. Take a look at the following example.

```
try:
    num1 = 10
    num2 = 0
    result = num1/num2
    print(result)
except Exception:
    print ("Sorry, program cannot continue")
else:
    print("Program executed without an exception")
```

In the script above, all the different types of exceptions will be handled by code block for Exception object. Therefore, a generic message will be printed to the user. In the script above, the num2 contains zero. Therefore, the "ZeroDivisionError" exception will occur. The result will look like this:

```
Sorry, program cannot continue
```

What's next?

In this chapter we studies how we can handle exceptions in Python. In the next chapter we will see how to perform file handling tasks with Python. Happy Coding!!!

Chapter 10

Python File Handling

File handling refers to performing variety of operations on different types of file. The most common file handling operations are opening a file, reading file contents, creating a file, writing data to a file, appending data to a file etc. Like every other programming language, Python supports almost all the major file handling functions. In this chapter, we will study how file handling can be achieved with Python.

Opening a File

Before you perform any function on a file, you need to open it. To open a file in python the **open** function is used. It takes 3 parameters: The path to the file, the mode in which the file should be opened and the buffer size in number of lines. The third parameter is optional. The **open** function returns file object. The syntax of the **open** function is as follows:

```
file_object = open(file_name,
file_mode, buffer_size)
```

Take a look at the following table for different types of modes along with their description:

Mode	Description
R	Opens file for read only
r+	Opens file for reading and writing
Rb	Only Read file in binary
rb+	Opens file to read and write in binary

W	Opens file to write only. Overwrites existing files with same name
Wb	Opens file to write only in binary. Overwrites existing files with same name
w+	Opens file for reading and writing
Wb	Opens file to read and write in binary. Overwrites existing files with same name
A	Opens a file for appending content at the end of the file
a+	Opens file for appending as well as reading content
Ab	Opens a file for appending content in binary
ab+	Opens a file for reading and appending content in binary

The file object returned by the *open* method has three main attributes:

1- name: returns the name of the file
2- mode: returns the mode with which the file was opened
3- closed: is the file closed or not

Take a look at the following example:

Note: Before you execute the script above, create a file ***test.txt*** and place it in the root directory of the D drive.

```
file_object                    =
open("D:/test.txt", "r+")
print(file_object.name)
print(file_object.mode)
print(file_object.closed)
```

In the script above, we open the test.txt file in the read and write mode. Next we print the name and mode of the file on the screen. Finally we print whether the file is closed or not. The output of the script above looks like this:

```
D:/test.txt
r+
False
```

To close an opened file, you can use ***close*** method. Take a look at the following example:

```
file_object                =
open("D:/test.txt", "r+")
print(file_object.name)
print(file_object.closed)
file_object.close()
print(file_object.closed)
```

In the script above, the test.txt file is opened in r+ mode. The name of the file is printed. Next we check if the file is opened using closed attribute, which returns false, since the file is open at the moment. We then close the file using close method. We again check if the file is closed, which returns true since we have closed the file. The output looks like this:

```
D:/test.txt
False
True
```

Writing Data to a File

To write data to a file, the **write** function is used. The content that is to be written to the file is passed as parameter to the write function. Take a look at the following example:

```
file_object              =
open("D:/test1.txt", "w+")

file_object .write( "Welcome
to      Python.\nThe     best
programming language!\n");


file_object .close()
```

In the script above, the file test.txt located at the root directory of D drive is opened. The file is opened for reading and writing. Next two lines of text have been passed to the write function. Finally the file is closed.

If you go to root directory of D drive, you will see a new file test1.txt with the following contents:

```
Welcome to Python.
The best programming language!
```

Reading Data from a File

To read data from a file in Python, the **read** function is used. The number of bytes to read from a file is passed as a parameter to the read function. Take a look at the following example:

```
file_object                =
open("D:/test1.txt", "r+")
sen = file_object.read(12)
print("The file reads: "+sen)


file_object .close()
```

The script above reads the first 12 characters from the test1.txt file that we wrote in the last example. The output looks like this:

```
The file reads: Welcome to P
```

To read the complete file, do not pass anything to the read function. The following script reads the complete test1.txt file and prints its content on the console:

```
file_object                =
open("D:/test1.txt", "r+")
sen = file_object.read()
```

```
print(sen)
file_object .close()
```

The output of the script above looks like this:

```
Welcome to Python.
The best programming language!
```

Renaming and Deleting Python Files

You can rename and delete python files using Python *os* module. To rename a file, the *rename* function is used. The old name of the file is passed as first parameter while new name is passed as second parameter. Take a look at the following example:

```
import os
os.rename(      "D:/test1.txt",
"D:/test2.txt" )
```

The above script renames file test1.txt to test2.txt

To delete a file in Python, the *remove* method is used. Take a look at the following example:

```
import os
```

```
os.remove("D:/test.txt")
```

The above script deletes the test.txt file located at the root directory of D drive.

File Positioning

To find the current position of the cursor in file, the *tell* function is used. Take a look at the following example:

```
file_object                    =
open("D:/test2.txt", "r+")
print(file_object.tell())
sen = file_object.read(12)
print(sen)
print(file_object.tell())
file_object .close()
```

In the script above, file test2.txt is opened. We then use to check the current position of the file, which returns 0. Next, the first 12 characters of the file are read. Next, the *tell* function is again called to find the current position of the file cursor. This time it will return 12, since the 12 characters have been just read using the read function. The output looks like this:

```
0
Welcome to P
12
```

What's Next?

In this chapter we studied how files are handled in Python. What the different file handling functions are and how to implement them. In the next chapter we will start our discussion about Functions in Python.

Chapter 11

Functions in Python

If a program has a large piece of code that is required to be executed repeatedly, it is better to implement that piece of code as a function and then call it using a loop. Functions foster code reusability, modularity and integrity. Consider a scenario where you have to add two numbers 100 times. Without function you will have assign values to two variables 100 times, perform the addition and print the result on console. If you are asked to perform subtraction, you will again have to change the plus sign into minus 100 times. In such a scenario, it is more convenient to write a function that accepts two numbers and performs addition between them. The function can then be called inside a loop. Similarly, if you to change addition to subtraction, you will have to do it at one place.

In this article we will see how to declare Python functions, how to call them, how to return values from them and some other operations.

Function Declaration

The syntax to create a function is as follows:

```
def function_name ():
      #code line 1
      #code line 2
      #code line 3
```

The function declaration starts with **def** keyword followed by the name of the function and opening and closing parenthesis. The parentheses are used for passing information to the function.

Let's write a simple function that prints 'Welcome to Python" on screen.

```
def print_welcome():
    print("Welcome to Python")
```

The above script creates a function named ***print_welcome*** . Function declaration completes successfully even if the function body contains errors. This is because a function body is actually evaluated when the function is called.

To call a function, simply type the name of the function followed by pair of parenthesis as shown below:

```
 Print_welcome()
```

When the above script executes, the print_welcome function executes and prints

"Welcome to Python" on the console. The output looks like this:

```
Welcome to Python
```

Parameterized Functions

In the previous example we left the parenthesis that follow the function name, empty. However these opening and closing parenthesis are used to pass parameters to function. Take a look at the following example:

```
def print_name(name):
    print("Person name :" + name)


print_name("James")
print_name("Sofia")
print_name("Rick")
```

In the script above, we define a function **_print_name_** which accepts one parameter name and print it inside the function.

In the function call to the print_name function, we pass the value for the name parameter. We call the print_name function thrice with three different values for the parameter. In the output you will see these values as follows:

```
Person name :James
Person name :Sofia
Person name :Rick
```

A function can have as many parameters as you want. However the sequence of parameters in the function definition must match the sequence in the function call. Take a look at the following function. It accepts three parameters: name, age and gender.

```
def print_details(name, age,
gender):
    print("Person name :" +
name)
```

```
    print("Person age :" +
str(age))
    print("Person gender :" +
gender)
    print("--------------------
")


print_name("James", 20,
"Male")
print_name("Sofia", 30,
"Female")
print_name("Rick", 25, "Male")
```

In the script above, we create a function *print_details.* The function accepts three parameters name, age and gender and prints them on the console. The function has been called thrice with different values for name, age and gender parameters. The output of the above script looks like this:

```
Person name :James
Person age :20
Person gender :Male
--------------------
Person name :Sofia
Person age :30
Person gender :Female
--------------------
Person name :Rick
Person age :25
Person gender :Male
--------------------
```

Returning Values from a Function

Just as you can pass information to a function via arguments (parameters, you can also return values from a function. To return value from a function the **return** keyword is used. Take a look at the following example.

```
def add_number(num1, num2):
    result = num1 + num2
    return result


result = add_number(10,20)
```

```
print("sum of 10 and 20 is :"
+ str(result))


result = add_number(5,15)
print("sum of 5 and 15 is :" +
str(result))
```

In the above script, we create a function *add_number.* The function accepts two arguments, adds them and returns the resultant sum.

We then call the function twice and pass it two different numbers. The result is printed on the console. The output looks like this:

```
sum of 10 and 20 is :30
sum of 5 and 15 is :20
```

Default Arguments

Python functions can have default values for the parameters, called default arguments. If no argument value is passed for that parameter from the function call, the default value is used. Take a look at the following script:

```
def add_number(num1, num2 =
100):

    result = num1 + num2

    return result


result = add_number(20)

print("sum of 100 and 20 is :"
+ str(result))


result = add_number(5,15)

print("sum of 5 and 15 is :" +
str(result))
```

In the script above we create an
add_number function. The num2 parameter
of the function has default argument value
of 100.

The add_number function is called twice. In
the first call only one argument is passed i.e.
20. This argument is passed for the num1
parameter. No argument is passed for the
num2 parameter. Therefore the default

argument value of 100 will be used and the returned result will be 120 (100 + 20).

In the second call to the add_number function, arguments for both num1 and num2 parameters have been passed. Therefore the default argument for num2 i.e. 100 will not be used. The result of the script above looks like this:

Passed by Value or By Reference?

Arguments passed to Python functions are by reference. That means that if the function updates the value of an argument, the value is also updated outside the function. This will become clearer with the help of following example:

```
def update_list(newlist):
    newlist.append([20,25,30]);
    return


numlist = [5,10,15];
```

```
print ("Values before function
call", numlist)

update_list( numlist );
print ("Values after function
call", numlist)
```

In the script above, we create a function called ***update_list.*** The function accepts a list as parameter and appends another list to it as an item.

We create a list named numlist with 3 items. We then print this list on the console. The list is then passed as argument to the update_list function which appends another list to it as an item. We then print the numlist on the console again. The results show that though numlist list being printed outside the update_list function, the numlist contains the list appended by update_list function. This is because the reference of the numlist was passed to the update_list function. And update inside the function also caused

update to the actual list. The output looks
like this:

```
Values before function call [5, 10, 15]
Values after function call [5, 10, 15, [20, 25, 30]]
```

Anonymous Functions

You can also create anonymous functions in
Python using single line statement without
def keyword. The anonymous functions are
created using lambda expressions and
cannot contain multiple expressions.

Take a look at the following example to see
how anonymous functions work:

```
result = lambda num1, num2,
num3: num1 + num2 + num3;

print ("Sum of three values :
", result( 5, 15, 25 ))
print ("Sum of three values :
", result( 2, 4, 6 ))
```

In the script above we create an anonymous function that adds three numbers. The function is stored in a variable named result. The function can then be called using this variable. In the above script the function has been called twice with three different parameter values for the function call. The output of the script looks like this:

```
Sum of three values :   45
Sum of three values :   12
```

Local vs. Global Variables

Depending upon their scope, there are two types of variables in Python: Local and Global. Scope of a variable refers to the part of code where a variable can be assessed.

A variable declared inside a function is called a local variable. Local variables cannot be accessed outside the function. On the other hand, a global variable is not declared inside the function and can be accessed anywhere within a program. Take a look at the following example to see difference between global and local variable.

```
total_students = 10 # global
variable


def
passed_students(p_students):
    #accessing global variable
total_students inside function
    failed_students =
total_students - p_students
    #printing local variable
failed_students
    print("Failed Students: "
+ str(failed_students))


# Accessing global variable
outside function
print("Total students" +
str(total_students))
passed_students(6)
```

In the script above, we define a global variable ***total_students***. We then define a function ***passed_students.*** Inside the function we accessed global variable ***total_students***. The function also contains local variable ***failed_students***.

Outside the function we again access global variable **total_students** and call the **passed_students** function. We will see that the global variable can be successfully accessed within a function and outside the function. The output looks like this:

```
Total students10
Failed Students: 4
```

Now if you try to access the local variable ***failed_students*** outside the ***passed_students*** function as follows:

```
print(failed_students)
```

An exception will be thrown:

```
---------------------------------------------------------------------------
NameError                                 Traceback (most recent call last)
<ipython-input-19-7c75ab616d4e> in <module>()
     10 print("Total students" + str(total_students))
     11 passed_students(6)
---> 12 print(failed_students)

NameError: name 'failed_students' is not defined
```

The error shows that *"failed_students"* variable is not defined. In other words, it cannot be accessed outside the function in which it was declared.

What's Next?

In this chapter, we completed our discussion about Python function. We saw different ways of creating functions with the help of examples. In the next chapter, we will start our discussion about object oriented programming in Python. Happy Coding!!!

Chapter 12

Object Oriented Programming in Python

Object oriented programming (OOP) is a programming paradigm in which the application is implemented in the form of objects that imitate real world entities. Objects can have attributes, methods and properties. Anything that contains some information and can perform a function is a candidate of being implemented as an object in OOP. Consider a scenario where you have to develop a first person shooter game using object oriented programming. You have to think about the real world objects that have some information and can perform some functionality in the first person shooter game. Shooter himself is an object since shooter has a name, height, weight, nationality etc. and can perform functions like run, sit, stand, crawl etc. Similarly, gun is also an entity since gun can shoot, load, reload etc. In this chapter, we will start our discussion about object oriented programming in Python.

Classes

A class is a basic building block of object oriented programming. In simple words, a class serves as a blue print for an object. Another analogy between classes and object is that of map and house. You can tell by reading a map that how the house is structured, where the dining room is, how many rooms are there in the house and so on. You can use one map to build several similar houses. Similarly, one class can be used to create several similar objects.

Take a look at the following example to see how we can create a class in Python. Let's create a simple class person:

```
# Creates class Person
class Person:
```

```python
#create class attributes
name = "Jospeh"
age = 28
gender = "Male"
role = "Shooter"


#create class methods
def stand(self):
    print            ("Person
standing")


def sit(self):
    print    ("Person    is
sitting")
```

In the script above we create a class Person with four attributes and three methods. The attributes are name, age, gender and role while the methods are **stand** and **sit**. The class methods are basically functions but they are defined inside the class body. It is important to mention that class methods take self as first parameter by default. The literal *self* refers to the class that contains the method.

As discussed earlier, classes are merely blue prints, they are animated via objects. One class can have multiple objects.

Objects

In Python, everything is treated as an object. Python objects can be broadly divided into two categories:

1- Built in Objects
2- Custom Objects

Built in Objects

Built in objects are the objects belonging to primitive data types. For instance, when you assign an integer to a variable, basically an integer object is stored in that variable. Take a look at the following script:

```
#creates an integer type object
age

age = 28
```

```
type(age)
```

In the script above we create an integer object and assign it to age variable. We then check the type of age variable which returns int.

Custom Objects

Custom objects are the objects that implement custom classes. In the previous section we created a class Person. Let's create object of the Person class. Take a look at the following script:

```
person1 = Person()
```

To create custom object, you simply have to write the name of the class followed by a pair of parenthesis and assign it to a named entity (variable) which is *person1* in the above example. Now the object *person1* can be used to access the Person class attributes and methods.

To access class attributes or methods, you can use the object name followed by the dot operator and the name of the attribute or the method. Take a look at the following example:

```
#accessing attributes
f_name = person1.name
print(f_name)
#assessing methods
person1.stand()
```

In the script above, the name attribute of the Person class is accessed via person1 object and the assigned to the f_name variable. The f_name variable is then printed on the screen.

Similarly, the stand function is accessed which prints the statement "Person standing" on the console. The output of the script above looks like this:

```
Jospeh
Person standing
```

Constructor

"Constructor" is a method that executes when a class is instantiated. The processes of creating object of a class is also known as instantiation. To create a constructor in Python, the **_init_** method is used. Take a look at the following example to see constructor in action.

```
# Creates class Person
class Person:

    #create constructor
    def __init__(self):
        print("Class      object
created")

    #create class methods
    def stand(self):
        print               ("Person
standing")
```

In the script above, we again create class Person. But this time the class has a constructor which simply prints some text on the screen. The class also contains **stand** method.

Now, when you create the object of the Person class, the constructor will execute and you will see "Class object created" on the console screen. Execute the following script:

```
person1 = Person()
```

The output will be:

```
Class object created
```

Attributes

We know that a value assigned to named entity in Python is actually an object. By the same analogy, the attributes declared inside a class are also objects. This means that objects can contain nested objects. Let's create a primitive string type object and check what attributes the object contains. Take a look at the following script:

```
#Creates   a   string   object
message
```

```
message = "I love Python"
#find all attributes of message
object
print(dir(message))
```

In the script above we create a string object named "message". To find all the attributes of an object the **dir** method is used. The output of the above script looks like this:

```
['__add__', '__class__', '__contains__', '__delattr__', '__dir__', '__doc__', '__eq__', '__format__', '__ge__', '__getattribute__', '__getitem__', '__getnewargs__', '__gt__', '__hash__', '__init__', '__init_subclass__', '__iter__', '__le__', '__len__', '__lt__', '__mod__', '__mul__', '__ne__', '__new__', '__reduce__', '__reduce_ex__', '__repr__', '__rmod__', '__rmul__', '__setattr__', '__sizeof__', '__str__', '__subclasshook__', 'capitalize', 'casefold', 'center', 'count', 'encode', 'endswith', 'expandtabs', 'find', 'format', 'format_map', 'index', 'isalnum', 'isalpha', 'isdecimal', 'isdigit', 'isidentifier', 'islower', 'isnumeric', 'isprintable', 'isspace', 'istitle', 'isupper', 'join', 'ljust', 'lower', 'lstrip', 'maketrans', 'partition', 'replace', 'rfind', 'rindex', 'rjust', 'rpartition', 'rsplit', 'rstrip', 'split', 'splitlines', 'startswith', 'strip', 'swapcase', 'title', 'translate', 'upper', 'zfill']
```

Class Attributes vs. Instance Attributes

Python classes have two types of attributes: Class attributes and Instance attributes. The instance attributes are specific to the individual objects of a class and are not shared between the objects. On the other hand, class attributes are shared among all the instances (objects) of a class.

The instance attributes are defined inside a method while the class attributes are defined outside the method. Take a look at the following example to see difference between class and instance attributes.

164

```python
# Creates class Person
class Person:

#Creates class attribute
    person_count = 0

#Creates method with instance
attributes
    def     set_details(self,
name, age, gender):
        #initialize    instance
variables
        self.name = name
        self.age = name
        self.gender = name
        #increment      class
variables
        Person.person_count +=
1
        print("Details     for
person " +self.name + "  have
been stored")
```

In the script above, as usual we create Person class. The class contains one class attribute person_count and a method *set_details*. Inside the *set_details* method, three instance attributes are initialized with the values passed as arguments to the *set_details* method. Inside the method, the person_count attribute is incremented by one. Another difference you can see here is that inside a class, the class attribute is accessed via class name whereas the instance attributes are accessed via keyword *self*.

Let's create an object of Person class and call the *set_details* method on the object.

```
person1 = Person()
person1.set_details("John",
24, "Male")
print("Person    count    "    +
str(person1.person_count))
```

In the script above, we create person1 object of Person class. We then call the *set_details* method using the object and pass some arguments to the method. The method prints the name of the person on console. We then print the class attribute person_count on the screen which will display 1. The output of the script above looks like this:

```
Details for person John have been stored
Person count 1
```

Now, let's create another Person class object.

```
Person2 = Person()
Person2.set_details("Suzi",
31, "Female")
print("Person    count    "    +
str(person2.person_count))
```

In the script above, we create person2 object of the Person class. This time, the shared attribute person_count will be incremented to 2 since it previously was 1.

The output of the script above looks like this:

```
Details for person Suzi have been stored
Person count 2
```

From the output you can see class attribute person_count is being shared between the two instances person1 and person2 while the instance attribute "name" is not being shared.

Properties

Encapsulation is one of the major building blocks of OOP. Encapsulation refers to providing controlled access to internal class data. The access is controlled via special methods. The special methods are bundled with the class attributes via properties and descriptors.

Why we need Properties?

In this section we will study properties. But first, let's see why we need properties.

Let's create a class named Medicine with three attributes: name, expiration_year and expiration_month. Execute the following script:

```
# Creates class Medicine
```

```python
class Medicine:

#Creates      Medicine      class
constructor
    def   __init__(self,  name,
expiry_year, expiry_month):
        #initialize    instance
variables


        self.name = name
        self.expiry_year       =
expiry_year
        self.expiry_month      =
expiry_month


    def getExpiryDate(self):
        print ('The expiration
date         is          :
'+str(self.expiry_month)+'/'+s
tr(self.expiry_year))
```

Now let's create an object of the Medicine
class.

```
medicine1   =   Medicine("xyz",
2020, 15)
```

In the script above, the constructor of the Medicine class assigns 15 as the month number to the expiry_month. To see the expiry date, call the **getExpiryDate** method using the medicine1 object as shown below:

```
medicine1.getExpiryDate()
```

Technically, any number can be assigned to the month. However, logically there are only 12 months in a year. So the number should be between 1 and 12. This is where properties come handy. Using properties you can control the value assigned and retrieved from the class members.

Take a look at the following script to see how properties can be created:

```
# Creates class Medicine
class Medicine:

#Creates     Medicine    class
constructor
```

```python
    def __init__(self, name,
expiry_year, expiry_month):
        #initialize    instance
variables

        self.name = name
        self.expiry_year    =
expiry_year
        self.expiry_month    =
expiry_month


    #Creates        expiry_month
property
    @property
    def expiry_month(self):
        return
self.__expiry_month


    #Create property setter
    @expiry_month.setter
    def    expiry_month(self,
expiry_month):
        if expiry_month < 1:
```

```python
            self.__expiry_month = 1
        elif    expiry_month    >
12:

            self.__expiry_month = 12
        else:

            self.__expiry_month       =
expiry_month


    def getExpiryDate(self):
        print ('The expiration
date            is              :
'+str(self.expiry_month)+'/'+s
tr(self.expiry_year))
```

To create a property for an attribute, you have to create method with the same name as the name of the attribute. For instance in the above script we wanted to create "expiry_month" property, therefore we created a method "expiry_month" and inside the method we return the value for "expiry_month" attribute using self and double underscore syntax. Remember that the property method must be decorated with the **@property** literal as shown in the script above.

Once the property is created, the next step is to set the rules on the property. Property setter is used for this purpose. The following script sets the rule on the "expiry_month" property.

```
#Create property setter
    @expiry_month.setter
    def     expiry_month(self,
expiry_month):
        if expiry_month < 1:

self.__expiry_month = 1
        elif  expiry_month  >
12:

self.__expiry_month = 12
        else:

self.__expiry_month         =
expiry_month
```

The logic implemented by the above script is simple. If the value assigned to the expiry_month is less than 1, then assign 1 to the expiry_month attribute. Else if the value assigned is greater than 12, assign 12 to the expiry_month variable. Finally, if the value assigned is between 1 and 12, assign that value.

Execute the following script:

```
medicine1  =  Medicine("xyz",
2020, 15)
medicine1.getExpiryDate()
```

In the script above, we create medicine1 object of Medicine class. Using the constructor, 15 is assigned as the value for expiry_month attribute. But since we have an expiry_month property, 12 will be assigned to the expiry_month attribute. If you call the **getExpiryDate** method, you will see 12 as expiry_month as shown in the output below:

```
The expiration date is : 12/2020
```

Static Methods

Class methods are similar to functions with
two major differences. Class methods are
defined inside class body. Class methods
take "self" as the first parameter. In this
chapter we have seen several examples of
instance methods. Instance methods are the
methods that are called via class object.
There is another category of methods that
can be called using class name. These
methods are called static methods. Take a
look at the following example to see static
methods in action:

```
#Creates Person Class
class Person:


    @staticmethod
    def run():
        print    ("Person    is
running")
```

```
def stand(self):
    print ("Person    is
standing")
```

In the script above, we create a class Person with one static method **_run_** and with one non static method **_stand_**. There are two differences between a static and non-static method in Python. A static method has to be decorated with **_@staticmethod_** decorator. On the other hand, non-static method doesn't require any decorator. Similarly, a static method doesn't need **_self_** as first parameter while the non-static method requires **_self_** as first parameter.

Let's call the static method **_run_** via Person class.

```
Person.run()
```

The output of the script above looks like this:

```
Person is running
```

Special Methods

Special methods or Magic methods are used to add special functionality to a class. The name of a special method starts and ends with double underscores. The constructor ___init___ is also a type of special methods. Other examples of special methods include str, del etc.

Primitive objects also contain special methods. For instance, **int** object contains ___add___ method which adds two integers. Take a look at the following example:

```
#Adding two numbers
int.__add__(15, 30)
```

The output of the above script will be 45.

The ___add___ method

Special methods can be overridden. For instance you can override ___add___ special method to add two or more custom classes. Take a look at the following example to see special Methods in action.

```
# Creates class Person
class Person:
```

```
#Creates method with instance
attributes
    def __init__(self, age):
        #initialize instance
variables
        self.age = age

#Overriding __add__ special
method
    def __add__(self, other):
        return self.age +
other.age
```

In the script above, we create a class named Person. The class has one attribute age which is initialized via constructor. The **__add__** method is overridden inside the Person class to add the age attribute of this class with the age attribute of the class object passed to the right side of the "+" operator.

Now when the two objects of the Person class are added via the "+" operator, actually the values for the age attributes of the objects will be added. Take a look at the following script:

```
person1 = Person(10)
person2 = Person(20)
sum_of_age = person1 + person2
print(sum_of_age)
```

In the script, 30 will be printed on the screen since sum of the age of person1 and person2 objects is 30.

The __gt__ method

The __gt__ special method is used to compare two or more classes for comparison. If the attribute of the class on the rleft hand side of the ">" is greater than the attribute of the class on the right hand side, the __gt__ method returns true, else it returns false. Let's modify our Person class to override the __gt__ method for the comparison of age attribute. Take a look at the following script:

```python
# Creates class Person
class Person:


#Creates method with instance
attributes
    def __init__(self, age):
        #initialize instance
variables
        self.age = age


#Overriding __add__ special
method
    def __add__(self, other):
        return self.age +
other.age


#Overriding __gt__ special
method
    def __gt__(self, other):
        return self.age >
other.age
```

Now, let's create two objects of Person class again and compare their age using ">" operator. Take a look at the following script:

```
person1 = Person(10)
person2 = Person(20)
person1 > person2
```

The value for person1 age attribute is 10 while the value for person2 age attribute is 20. Next, person1 object is being compared to person2 object using ">" operator. But since person1 object's age attribute is less than person2's age attribute, False will be returned.

The __str__ method

The __*str*__ method is called when the object is used as string. For instance when you pass the object to print method, the __*str*__ method of the object executes. Like any other special methods, the __*str*__ method can also be overridden. Take a look at the following example to see how we can override ___*str*___ method of the Person class so that it prints the name of the Person.

```
# Creates class Person
class Person:



#Creates method with instance
attributes
    def __init__(self, name):
        #initialize    instance
variables
        self.name = name


    def __str__(self,):
        return "The person is
" + self.name
```

Let's create object of the Person class and try to print on the console:

```
person1 = Person("James")
print(person1)
```

When the script above is executed, the **_str_** method of the Person class executes which produces following output:

```
The person is James
```

Local vs. Global Variables

Like instance and class attributes, variables in Python also have two types: Global variables and local variables. Any variable defined outside the function body is called global variable while variable defined inside the function body is called local variable. Take a look at the following example to see local and global variables in action:

```
#declare global variable
count = 1;

def print_count():
    #Accessing global variable
    print("Accessing    global
variable inside function :" +
str(count))
    num = 2;
```

```
print(count)
print_count()
print(num)
```

In the script above, we first declare a global variable count. The global variable is then accessed inside the **_print_count_** function. Inside the function a local variable "num' is also declared.

Finally, global variable "count" and local variable "num" are accessed outside the function. You will see that the above code will return an error since "num" is a local variable and cannot be accessed outside the **_print_count_** function. The output of the above script looks like this:

```
--------------------------------------------------------------------------
NameError                                Traceback (most recent call last)
<ipython-input-49-2c4ee615bb26> in <module>()
     10 print(count)
     11 increment_count()
---> 12 print(num)

NameError: name 'num' is not defined
```

You can see that since we tried to access the local variable "num" outside the function, an error was thrown that "num" is not defined.

Modifiers

Modifiers in Python are used to specify the scope of a variable. Like most of the other programming languages, Python has three access modifiers: Public, Private and Protected. Variables with Public access modifier can be accessed anywhere within the program. Public variables names do not have leading underscore before their names. On the other hand, variables with private modifiers can only be accessed within the class. Private variable names start with double underscore. Finally, protected variables can be accessed within the class and within the child classes (We will see parent child classes in the next chapter).

Take a look at the following example to see Modifiers in action:

```
#Creating Person Class
class Person:
```

```python
    def __init__(self, name,
age, gender):
        #Private Variable
        self.__age = age
        #Public Variable
        self.name = name
        #Protected Variable
        self._gender = gender
```

In the script above we have a Person class with three instance variables: name, age and gender. The name variable is public; age variable is private while the gender variable is protected.

Let's create an object of the Person class and try to access the variables outside the person class. Take a look at the following script:

```python
person1 = Person("John", 20,
"Male")
#accessing public variable
print(person1.name)
```

```
#accessing private variable
print(person1.age)
```

In the script above we first access the public variable name via the person1 object of the Person class. We then access the private variable age of the Person class. In the output you will see that we will be able to access the name variable since it is public but an error will be thrown when we try to access private variable age, outside the Person class. The output of the script looks like this:

```
John
----------------------------------------------------------------------
AttributeError                          Traceback (most recent call last)
<ipython-input-58-344f0af8bdac> in <module>()
      3 print(person1.name)
      4 #accessing private variable
----> 5 print(person1.age)

AttributeError: 'Person' object has no attribute 'age'
```

The error says that Person object has no attribute age. This is because age is private and cannot be accessed outside the Person class.

Conclusion & What's Next?

In this chapter we started our discussion about Object Oriented Programming in Python. We saw different OOP concepts including classes, objects, attributes, methods, modifiers etc. In the next chapter we will study what is Inheritance and how it is implemented in Python. Happy Coding!!!

Chapter 13

Inheritance & Polymorphism

In the previous chapter we started our discussion about object programming (OOP) and covered most of the basic OOP concepts. There are three pillars of OOP: data encapsulation, inheritance and polymorphism. In the previous chapter we studied how access modifiers and properties are used to implement data encapsulation in Python. In this chapter we will study inheritance and polymorphism.

Inheritance Basics

Inheritance in programming refers to the ability of a class to inherit methods and attributes of other classes. This is similar to real world inheritance. A child inherits some of the characteristics of her parents; in addition to her own unique characteristics. A class that inherits another class is called child class or derived class and the class that is inherited by another class is called parent or base class.

The child and parent classes have is "IS-A" between them. For instance a child class car is a vehicle which is its parent class. Similarly, employee is a person. As a rule of thumb, if multiple classes have some common methods and attributes, a parent class should be defined that contains those methods and attributes. The parent class can then be inherited by the multiple child classes. This will be clear with the help of an example.

Let's create a simple class named "Parent" with one method. We will also create a class named child that inherits the "Parent" class.

```
#Create Class Parent
class Parent:
    def methodA (self):
        print("Hello, I am a
Parent class method")
```

```
#Create    Class    Child    that
inherits Parent
class Child(Parent):
    def methodB (self):
        print("Hello, I am a
Child class method")


#Create object of class Child
child = Child()
#Access Parent class method
child.methodA()
#Access Child class method
child.methodB()
```

In the script above we create a Parent class
and a Child class. The Child class inherits the
Parent class. To inherit a class, you just have
to pass the parent class name inside the
parenthesis that follow the child class name.
In the above script Parent class contains a
method named ***methodA***, while the child
class also contains a method named
methodB. We then create a child class object

named "child". From this "child" object we call the **methodA**. You can see that though Child class doesn't contain **methodA**, but since it is inheriting Parent class which contains **methodA**, therefore the Child class object can also access this method. Finally we call the Child class method **methodB.** The output of the script above looks like this:

```
Hello, I am a Parent class method
Hello, I am a Child class method
```

Like methods, the child class also inherits attributes from parent class. Take a look at the following example:

```
#Create Class Parent
class Parent:
    name =""
    age = ""
    def methodA (self):
        print("Hello, I am a
Parent class method")
```

```python
#Create    Class    Child    that
inherits Parent
class Child(Parent):
    def methodB (self):
        print("Hello,  I  am  a
Child class method")


#Create object of class Child
child = Child()
#Access Parent class method
child.methodA()
#Access Child class method
child.methodB()
#Access        parent        class
attributes
child.name = "Jacob"
child.age = 10
print(child.name  +  "  "  +
str(child.age))
```

In the script above, we have a parent class
with two attributes name and age, and one
method ***methodA***, in child class we access
the method and attributes and display their
values on the console.

Multiple Child Classes

Multiple child classes can inherit from a parent class. Take a look at the following script:

```python
#Create Class Parent
class Parent:
    def methodA (self):
        print("Hello, I am a Parent class method")


#Create Class Child1 that inherits Parent
class Child1(Parent):
    def methodB (self):
        print("Hello, I am a Child1 class method")


#Create Class Child2 that inherits Parent
class Child2(Parent):
    def methodC (self):
        print("Hello, I am a Child2 class method")
```

```
#Create  object of class Child1
child1 = Child1()
#Access Parent class method
child1.methodA()
#Access Child1 class method
child1.methodB()

#Create  object of class Child2
child2 = Child2()
#Access Parent class method
child2.methodA()
#Access Child1 class method
child2.methodC()
```

In the script above, we have two child classes Child1 and Child2 that inherit the parent class named Parent. Both the child classes have now access to the Parent class method i.e. *methodA*, the output of the script above looks like this:

```
Hello, I am a Parent class method
Hello, I am a Child1 class method
Hello, I am a Parent class method
Hello, I am a Child2 class method
```

Calling Parent Class Constructor from Child Class

We know that a class inherits parent class and its attributes. But a question arises here that how can we initialize the attributes of the parent class using child class constructors. For instance, if there are two attributes in the parent class and 1 attribute in the child class. How do we initialize these three attributes using child class constructor?

Python provides simple solution to this problem. The arguments for the parent and child class constructors are passed to the child class. Inside the child class constructor, the parent class constructor is called and arguments for the parent class constructor are passed to it. The remaining arguments are used to initialize the child class attributes. Take a look at the following example:

```
#Create Vehicle Class
class Vehicle:
    #Constructor    for    the
Parent class
    def __init__ (self, name,
color):
        self.name = name
        self.color = color



#Create    Bike    Class    that
inherits Vehicle Class
class Bike(Vehicle):
    #Constructor for the child
class
    def __init__ (self, name,
color, price):
        #Call to Vehicle class
Constructor from Bike class
        Vehicle.__init__
(self, name, color)
        self.price = price
```

```
#Create Vehicle Class Object
bike                          =
Bike("Honda","Black",25000)
#Access       parent       class
attributes
print(bike.name)
print(bike.color)
#Access child class attribute
print(bike.price)
```

In the script above we create Parent class "Vehicle" with two attributes: name and color. The parent class constructor initializes these two attributes. We then defined a child class "Bike" that inherits class Vehicle. Child class has one attribute i.e. price which is initialized via child Bike class constructor. However the Bike class constructor takes three parameters name, color and age. Inside the Bike class constructor, the Vehicle class constructor is called and the name and color attributes are passed to Vehicle class constructor. While the price argument is used to initialize the child class attribute price.

We create object of the Bike class and pass it values for name, color and price attributes. We then print these values on the console. The output of the above script looks like this:

```
Honda
Black
25000
```

Multiple Inheritance

We know that a parent class can be inherited by multiple child classes. This is the type of inheritance supported by programming languages like Java and C#. However, in Python, one child class can also inherit multiple parent classes. This is called multiple inheritance.

The following example will further clear the concept of multiple inheritance.

```
class Vehicle:
    def     showVehicleDetails
(self):
```

```python
        print("I    am    vehicle
class")


class Sedan:
    def        showSedanDetails
(self):
        print("I    am    sedan
class")


#Create Class Car that inherits
Vehicle and Sedan
class Car(Vehicle,Sedan):
    def showCarDetails (self):
        print("I    am    car
class")


#Create object of car Class
car = Car()
#Access Vehicle class method
car.showVehicleDetails()
#Access Sedan class method
car.showSedanDetails()
#Access child class method
```

```
car.showCarDetails()
```

In the script above we have three classes Vehicle, Sedan and Car. The Car class inherits both Vehicle and Sedan class. We then create the object of the Car class and access the Vehicle and Sedan class methods from the car class object. The example shows that a child class that inherits multiple parents has access to all the attributes and methods of all the parent classes. The output of the above example looks like this:

```
I am vehicle class
I am sedan class
I am car class
```

Method Overriding

In addition to having access to parent class methods, a child class can also override parent class method by providing its own definition for the same method name. Take a look at the following example to understand this concept:

```
#Create Person Class
class Employee:

    def printdetails (self):

        print("I       am       an
employee of this company")


#Create  Class  Manager  that
inherits Employee
class Manager(Employee):

    def printdetails (self):

        print("I  am  a  Manager
of this company")


manager = Manager()
manager.printdetails()
```

In the script above, we created two classes:
Employee and Manager. The Employee class
contains a method *printdetails.* The
Manager class inherits the Employee class
which means that the Manager class has
access to the *printdetails* method of the
Employee class. However in the Manager
contains its own definition of the
printdetails method. Now when you create

the object of the Manager class and call the **printdetails** method, the method that is overridden in the child class will be called instead of the parent class method as shown in the following output:

```
I am a Manager of this company
```

Polymorphism

The world polymorphism literally refers to "ability to adopt multiple shapes". In programming, polymorphism refers to the capability of a method to behave differently depending upon different scenarios such as number and type of parameters of a method and the type of object that calls the method(whether it is child or parent class object)

A simple example of polymorphism is the addition operator. When you use addition operator to add two numbers, the addition operator works like mathematical addition operator and returns the sum of the operands. However, if the same addition operator is used to add two string, the resultant value is a concatenated string. Take a look at a simple example:

```
#Using  addition  operator  for
sum
x = 10
y = 20

result = x + y
print(result)

#using  addition  operator  for
string concatenation

x = "Welcome"
y = "to Python"

result = x + y
print(result)
```

In the script above we assign two numeric values to variables x and y. We then use addition operator to add these values and store the sum in the result variable. We then print the result variable on screen which is a numeric variable. This shows that addition operator adds two numeric operands. Next, we assign two string type values to x and y variables and again use addition operator. This time the addition operator concatenates two strings. The example shows how addition operator follows polymorphism depending upon the operands.

In custom classes, polymorphism is implemented via method overloading and method overriding. We studied method overriding in the previous section, here we shall see method overloading.

Method overloading refers to the ability of a method to perform different function based on the arguments passed to it. Take a look at a simple example of method overloading:

```
#Create Employee
class Employee:
    def printname (self, name
= None):
```

```
        if name == None:
            print("Hello, I am
an employee")
        else:
            print("Hello, I am
an employee. My name is ",name)
```

In the script above we create a class Employee with one method ***printname***. The ***printname*** method has one optional parameter i.e. name. The ***printname*** method can be called with one string type argument or without any argument. If the method is called with no argument, the statement "Hello, I am an employee" will be printed on the console. If the ***printname*** method is called with a string type argument, the statement "Hello, I am an employee. My name is ",name" will be printed on the screen with the argument replacing the name variable. Let's create an object of Employee class and call the ***printname*** method with and without any argument.

```
emp = Employee()
```

```
emp.printname()
emp.printname("Joseph")
```

The output of the above script looks like this:

```
Hello, I am an employee
Hello, I am an employee. My name is  Joseph
```

Conclusion and What's Next?

In this chapter we studied two of the most important OOP concepts i.e. inheritance and polymorphism. With this, we have covered most of the basic as well as advanced Python programming concepts that you will need to develop Python applications. In the next and final chapter, we will study another some other extremely useful tools for programming in Python i.e. Lambda operator and List Comprehensions.

Chapter 14

Lambda Operators and List Comprehensions

In Chapter 11 (Functions in Python) of this book, we studied how we can create lambda functions or anonymous functions in one line of code. However, lambda operator is not merely used to create anonymous functions. There are many other uses of lambda operators which we will study in this chapter.

Mostly, the lambda operator is used in combination with map(), reduce() and filter() operations. We will see the detail of each of these filters in detail, but first let's revise how to create a simple lambda function.

Take a look at a simple example:

```
sum = lambda a,b,c: a + b + c
result = sum(10,15,5)
print(result)
```

In the script above we create a lambda function with three parameters a, b and c. The function adds these three parameters and returns the sum. The function is stored in sum variable. The function can now be called using the sum variable name. We then call the function by passing three numeric arguments to the sum variable and print the result on the screen. The output of the above expression will be 10 + 15 + 5 = 20.

The Map Function

The map function is used to apply a function on a sequence and return updated sequence. The map function takes (1) function to apply as first argument and (2) sequence to be updated as the second argument. The map function returns map type object which can be parsed into list using list function. Take a look at the following example:

```
def takesquare(x):
    return(x * x)


nums = [2,4,6,8,10]


squares  =  map(takesquare,
nums)
print(list(squares))
```

In the script above we create function *takesquare* which takes one parameter and returns square of the value passed as parameter. The function here applies on only one parameter, however using map function, we can apply this function to each individual element of the list. Next in the above script we create a list of even numbers from 2 to 10. Next, we use map function and pass it *takesquare* function as first argument, and the list "nums" as second argument. The map function will apply *takesquare* function on individual element of the list, for instance 2 will be squared to 4, 4 will be squared to 16 and so on. The resultant sequence is stored in the "squares" variable. We then convert the squares object to list and print it on the console. The output will look like this:

```
[4, 16, 36, 64, 100]
```

In the script we did not use lambda function; we simply passed a concrete function. However, the real beauty of map function lies in its ability to use lambda functions. Take a look at the following example:

```
squares2 = map(lambda x: x*x, nums)
print(list(squares2))
```

In the script above, we have a map function that uses lambda function to take square of value passed to it and apply this function on the sequence. The output will be similar to that of the previous script:

```
[4, 16, 36, 64, 100]
```

You can even use two or more than two sequences in the map function and apply some functionality on both of the lists, simultaneously. Take a look at the following script:

```
even = [2,4,6,8,10]
odd =  [1,3,5,7,9]
result = map(lambda a,b: a+b,
even, odd)
print(list(result))
```

In the script above we have two lists. One contains even numbers from 2 to 10 and the other contains odd numbers from 1 to 7. The map function adds the contents of the list. It is important to mention here that the size of all the sequences in the map function should be equal.

The Filter Function

The filter function also takes two parameters: function and sequence. It returns the items from the sequence for which the function returns true and ignores the remaining items in the sequence. Take a look at a simple example of filter function:

```
nums = [1,2,3,4,5,6,7,8,9,10]
result = filter(lambda a: a %
2 == 0, nums)
print(list(result))
```

In the script above, we have a list of numbers from 1 to 10. In filter function we have a lambda function which returns true if number is divisible by 2. Hence all the even numbers from the nums list will be returned. The output of the script above looks like this:

```
[2, 4, 6, 8, 10]
```

The Reduce Function

The reduce function, like the map and filter functions, take two parameters: function and sequence. However, unlike map and filter functions, the reduce function returns single element. The working of reduce function is simple; it starts by applying the function to the first two elements of the sequence. The function is again applied to the result of the previous function and the third value in the sequence. The process continues until all the values in the sequence are iterated.

This is best explained with the help of an example:

```
from functools import reduce
nums = [2,4,6,8,10]
result = reduce(lambda a,b:
a*b, nums)
print(result)
```

To use reduce function you need to import if first. In the script above the reduce function takes produce of all the even numbers from 2 to 10. The reduce function works by first multiplying 2 and 4. It then multiplies the product of 2 and 4 with the third element i.e. 6 and so on. In the output you will see 3840 i.e. the produce of all the numbers in the nums list.

List Comprehensions

List comprehensions can be used to create lists using set notation. List comprehensions can be used to simplify tasks performed by map and reduce functions. Take a look at a simple example of list comprehension where list of integers is converted into corresponding list of squares of integers.

```
evens = [2,4,6,8,10]
squares = [x*x for x in evens]
print(squares)
```

The above script takes squares of all the even numbers in the evens list and prints them on the console. The output will look like this:

```
[4, 16, 36, 64, 100]
```

Similarly, you can filter items from a list using list comprehension. Take a look at the following example.

```
nums = [1,2,3,4,5,6,7,8,9,10]
evens = [x for x in nums if x
% 2 == 0]
print(evens)
```

The script above filters all the even numbers from the nums list and display them on the console.

List comprehensions can also be used to find cross products of two sets of elements. Take a look at the following example:

```
sizes = ['Short', 'Medium',
'Large', 'X-Large' ]
persons = ['Men', 'Women',
'Boy', 'Girl']
cp = [(a,b) for a in sizes for
b in persons]
print(cp)
```

In the script above we have two sets in the form of list. The sizes list contains for different sizes while the persons list contains different types of persons. We take the cross product of two lists using list notations and store the result in the "cp" variable which is subsequently printed on the console. The cross product of the sizes and persons list looks like this:

```
[('Short', 'Men'), ('Short', 'Women'), ('Short', 'Boy'), ('Short', 'Girl'), ('Medium', 'Men'), ('Mediu
m', 'Women'), ('Medium', 'Boy'), ('Medium', 'Girl'), ('Large', 'Men'), ('Large', 'Women'), ('Large',
'Boy'), ('Large', 'Girl'), ('X-Large', 'Men'), ('X-Large', 'Women'), ('X-Large', 'Boy'), ('X-Large',
'Girl')]
```

Conclusion and What's Next

In this chapter we completed our discussion on lambda operators and list comprehensions. This chapter marks the end of this book. In this book we studied most of the basic and advanced Python concepts. With these concepts, you should be able to develop any Python applications with the help of different Python libraries. I would suggest that you practice the exercises in this book again and again and then start building small projects like calculator, tic tac toe or hangman game. Remember, you will learn as you program. Happy Coding!

FREE E-BOOK DOWNLOAD :

http://bit.ly/2yJsyq4

or

http://pragmaticsolutionstech.co
m/

Use the link above to get instant access
to the bestselling E-Book **Data
Analytics' Guide For Beginners**

rendering of legal, financial, medical or professional advice. Please consult a licensed professional before attempting any techniques outlined in this book.

By reading this document, the reader agrees that under no circumstances are is the author responsible for any losses, direct or indirect, which are incurred as a result of the use of information contained within this document, including, but not limited to, —errors, omissions, or inaccuracies.

Contents

William Sullivan

FREE E-BOOK DOWNLOAD :

http://bit.ly/2yJsyq4

or

http://pragmaticsolutionstech.com/

Use the link above to get instant access to the bestselling E-Book **Data Analytics' Guide For Beginners**

RESOURCES:

All the datasets that we are going to use in this book can be found at this link:

https://drive.google.com/file/d/1TB0tMuLv uL0Ad1dzHRyxBX9cseOhUs_4/view?usp=sh aring

Also, you can find all scripts used in the book within this link below:

https://drive.google.com/file/d/1qn9G-W7v2mXcTSxk9ejbqiHjD_pxat1U/view?usp=sha ring

Introduction

Machine learning is one of the hottest buzz words around. With the advancement in high computing hardware and availability of thousands of terra bytes of data, more and more companies and research organizations are using machine learning to build intelligent machines that can perform variety of tasks and can help humans make better decisions.

This book contains detailed overview of all the latest concepts in machine learning. Each chapter in this book is dedicated to one machine learning algorithm. Each chapter begins with the brief theory of the algorithm followed by implementation of the algorithm in Python's Scikit learn library.

The book is aimed towards novice as well as expert users. On hand it can be used as handbook of machine learning for the beginners, while on the other hand it can also be used by expert users as reference for different machine learning algorithms. To get out of this book, you are requested to not mere read the book but to actually hand code all the examples provided in this book.

In the end, I wish you best in your machine learning endeavors. I hope once you read this book, you have all the basic tools in your machine learning arsenal to solve any type of machine learning problem.

Chapter 1

Introduction to machine Learning

Machine learning is a branch of Artificial Intelligence that deals with learning implicitly from data using various statistical techniques. Unlike traditional computer programs where all the application logic is explicitly programed, machine learning applications learn implicitly from the data without being explicitly programmed. The idea behind machine learning is that instead of hard coded logic, large amount of data is fed into the application. It is then the responsibility of the application to learn from that data and make decisions.

Definition

The first definition of machine learning was coined by Arthur Samuel back in 1959. He defined machine learning as:

"Field of study that enables computers to learn without being explicitly programmed."

Tom Mitchel *from Carnegie Mellon University defined machine learning in mathematically understandable terms as in 1997. He said:*

"A computer program is said to learn from experience E with respect to some task T and some performance measure P, if its performance on T, as measured by P, improves with experience E."

The definition provided by Tom Mitchel is widely regarded as the most precise yet clear definition of machine learning. Now we know what machine learning is, but a question still remains that how machines learning and what is their inner working. The next section will answer this question:

How Machines Learn?

Before dwelling into the details of machine learning, let us first recapitulate that how humans learn. For instance, how we humans know that we should not touch a heating plates when they are on with bare hands. How we know that they can cause burns? Well there can be two possibilities: Either we have been burned in the past by heating stove or we have been taught by elders not to touch the heating plates. In both the cases we have had some experience in the past that stops us from touching heating plates when they are on. In other words, we had some past information, on the basis of which we make future decisions.

Machine learns in a similar way. In the beginning they have no knowledge. They are just like a newborn child with zero knowledge. To make machines learn, information is passed to these machines. From this information, machines identify patterns using various statistical techniques. Once machines learn to identify patterns from the data for making decisions, they can be used to make decisions on unseen data.

Workflow of a typical learning process of a machine learning model is shown in the following figure:

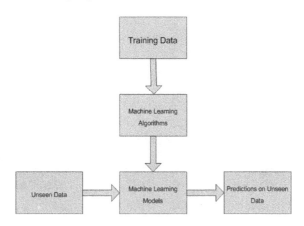

Training data is fed into machine learning algorithms that are nothing but complex mathematical algorithms. The algorithms results in machine learning models. Machine learning models are capable of making predictions on new unseen data which is also known as test data.

Importance of Machine Learning

The ultimate goal of AI is to make machines as intelligent as humans. However initial work in AI showed that we cannot hardcode machines that are as intelligent as humans. Humans learn from the environment which is consistently evolving. Therefore, the best way to make intelligent machines is to make them learn themselves. Therefore, machine learning was recognized as a discipline of science that teaches machines how to automatically learn from the data.

The idea behind machine learning is that instead of hardcoding the logic, data is fed into the machines and make machines themselves learn from the data by identifying patterns from the data. Interestingly machines learning techniques are quicker than humans in identifying patterns.

Machine learning techniques have been around for quite a while. However owing to the lack of high performance hardware, these techniques were not implemented before to solve real world problems. Now, with the availability of complex hardware and huge amount of data, machine learning techniques have resurfaced and have been successful in developing intelligent machines.

Types of Machine Learning

Machine learning techniques have been broadly categorized into two types:

1- Supervised Learning
2- Unsupervised Learning

1. Supervised Learning

In supervised learning, both the input data and the corresponding category that the input data belongs to is provided to the learning algorithm. The learning algorithm learns the relationship between the input and the output and then predicts the output of the unseen input data samples.

For instance, supervised machine learning algorithm is fed with images of apples labeled as fruit and potatoes labeled as vegetable. After training on this data, the supervised machine learning algorithm should be able to classify new unlabeled images of apples as fruit and unlabeled potatoes as vegetable.

Following are the steps involved in supervised machine learning algorithm:

1- Feed the algorithm with input records X, and output labels y.
2- For each input record the algorithm predicts an output y'.
3- Error in prediction is calculated by subtracting y from y'.
4- The algorithm corrects itself by removing the error.
5- Steps 1 to 4 continue for multiple iterations until error is minimized.

In mathematical terms, you have input variable X and output variable y, and you have to find a function that captures relationship between the two i.e.

$$y = f(X)$$

Supervised Learning is used to solve two different types of problems: classification and regression.

Classification: Classification refers to process of predicting discrete output values for an input. For instance, given an input predicting whether a mail is spam or ham, a tumor is benign or malignant or whether a student will pass or fail the exam.

Regression: In regression problems the task of machine learning model is to predict a continuous value. For instance for given input, predict the price of the house or predict the marks obtained by a student on an exam e.tc.

2. Unsupervised Learning

In supervised learning, the algorithms are fed with the input data with no labels. It is the responsibility of the algorithm to identify patterns in the data and cluster records with similar characteristics. Normally, most of the real world data is unlabeled; therefore unsupervised learning can be used as a precursor to supervised learning.

For instance, customers shopping trend can be fed into an unsupervised learning algorithm. The algorithm can find trends in the shopping. Consider a scenario where the algorithm finds that the customers who buy baby products also buy milk. Therefore, a business decision to place the milk close to the baby products can be based on this information.

Conclusion

In this chapter we introduced the machine learning as subject matter. We saw what machine learning is and what different types of machine learning are. The next chapter is dedicated to installing the software required to run machine learning algorithms in this chapter. We will be using Python's Scikit Learn Library for implementing different machine learning algorithms.

Chapter 2

Environment Setup

In this chapter we will install the software that we are going to use to run our Machine learning Programs. There are several options available to implement machine learning, however we will be using Python since most of the advanced machine learning community is working with Python for machine learning. To install Python several options available. You can simply install core Python and use a text editor like notepad to write Python programs. These programs can then be run via command line utilities. The other option is to install an Integrated Develop Environment (IDE) for Python. IDE provides a complete programming environment including Python installation, Editors and debugging tools. Most of the advanced programmers take the IDE route for Python development. We are also going to take the same route.

Anaconda is the IDE that we are going to use throughout this book. Anaconda is light, easy to install and comes with variety of development tools. Anaconda has its own command line utility to install third party software. And the good thing is that with Anaconda, you don't have to separately install Python environment.

Downloading and Installing Anaconda

Follow these steps to download and install anaconda. In this section we will show the process of installing Anaconda for windows. The installation process remains almost same for Linux and Mac.

11- Go to the following URL https://www.anaconda.com/downlo ad/

12- You will be presented with the following webpage. Select Python 3.6 version as this is currently the latest version of Python. Click the "Download" button to download the executable file. It takes 2-3 minutes to download the file depending upon the speed of your internet.

13- Once the executable file is downloaded, go to the download folder and run the executable. The name of the executable file should be similar to "Anaconda3-5.1.0-Windows-x86_64." When you run the file you will see installation wizard like the one in the following screenshot. Click "Next" button.

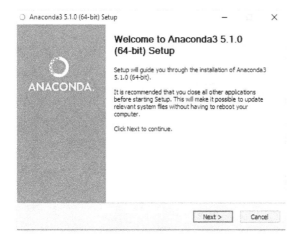

14- "License Agreement" dialogue box will appear. Read the license agreement and Click "I Agree" button.

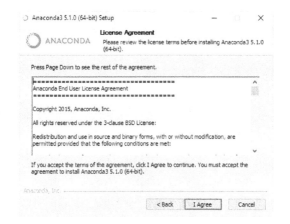

15- From the "Select Installation Type" dialogue box, check the "Just Me" radio button and click "Next" button as shown in the following screenshot.

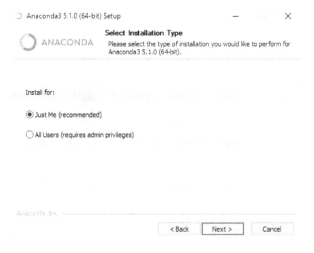

16- Choose the installation directory (Default is preferred) from the "Choose Install Location" dialogue box and click "Next" button. You should have around 3 GB of free space in your installation directory.

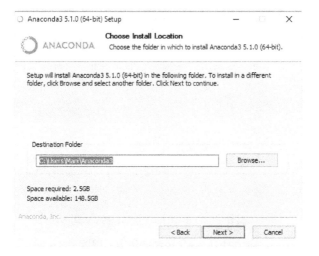

Anaconda3 5.1.0 (64-bit) Setup — □ ×

Choose Install Location

Choose the folder in which to install Anaconda3 5.1.0 (64-bit).

Setup will install Anaconda3 5.1.0 (64-bit) in the following folder. To install in a different folder, click Browse and select another folder. Click Next to continue.

Destination Folder

C:\Users\Mani\Anaconda3   Browse...

Space required: 2.5GB
Space available: 148.5GB

Anaconda, Inc.

< Back   Next >   Cancel

17- From the "Advanced Installation
Options" dialogue box, select the
second checkbox "Register Anaconda
as my default Python 3.6" and click
the "Install" button as shown in the
following screenshot.

The installation process will start which can take some time to complete. Sit back and enjoy a cup of coffee.

18- Once the installation completes, click the "Next" button as shown below.

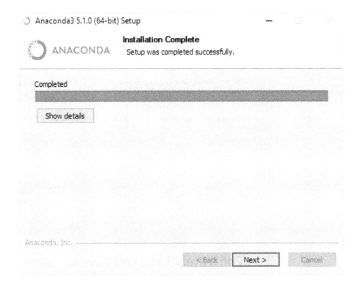

19- "Microsoft Visual Studio Code Installation" window appear, click "Skip" button.

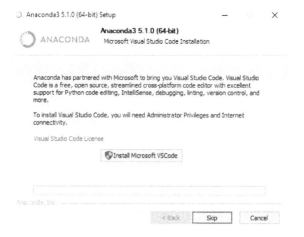

20- Congratulations, you have installed Anaconda. Uncheck the both the checkboxes on the dialogue box that appears and "Finish" button.

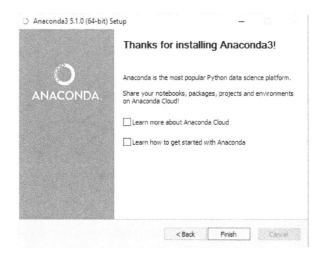

Running your First Program

We have installed environment required to run Python scripts. Now is the time to run our first program. With Anaconda, you have several ways to do so. We will see two of those in this section.

Go to your window search box and type "Anaconda Navigator" and then select the "Anaconda Navigator" application as shown below:

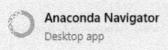

Anaconda Navigator
Desktop app

Folders

anaconda_navigator - in site-packages

anaconda_navigator - in site-packages

anaconda_navigator-1.7.0-py3.6.egg-info -
in site-packages

anaconda_navigator-1.7.0-py3.6.egg-info -
in site-packages

anaconda-navigator-1.7.0-py36_0

Search suggestions

🔎 Anaconda Navigator - See web results >

🔎 anaconda navigator **youtube** >

🔎 anaconda navigator **windows** >

🔎 anaconda navigator **download** >

🔎 anaconda navigator **app** >

🔎 Anaconda Navigator

Anaconda Navigator Dashboard will appear that looks like this.

Note: It takes some time for Anaconda Navigator to start, so be patient.

From the dashboard, you can see all of the tools available to develop your python applications. In this book we will mostly use "Jupyter Notebook" (second from top). Though in this chapter we shall also see how to run python script via "Spyder".

Running Scripts via Jupyter Notebook

Jupyter notebook runs in your default browser. From the navigator, launch "Jupyter Notebook" (Second option from the top).

Another way to launch Jupyter is by typing "Jupyter Notebook" in the search box and selecting the "Jupyter Notebook" application from the start menu as shown below:

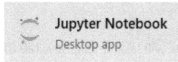
Jupyter Notebook
Desktop app

Folders

jupyter_notebook_config.d - in jupyter

jupyter_notebook_config.d - in jupyter

Documents

jupyter-notebook-script

jupyter_notebook_config

Search suggestions

jupyter notebook - See web results >

jupyter notebook download >

jupyter notebook login >

jupyter notebook online >

jupyter notebook app >

jupyter notebook images >

jupyter notebook

Jupyter notebook will launch in a new tab of your default browser.

To create a new notebook, click "new" button at the top-right corner of the Jupyter notebook dashboard. From dropdown, select "Python 3."

You will see new Python 3 notebook that looks like this:

Jupyter notebook consists of cells. Python script is written inside these cells. Let's print hello world using Jupyter notebook. In the first cell of the notebook enter "print('hello world') and press CTRL+ ENTER. The script in the first cell will be executed as shown below:

The "print" function prints the string passed to it as parameter, in the output. To create a new cell, click the "+" button from the top left menu as shown below:

You can write Python script in the new cell and press CTRL + ENTER to execute it.

Running Scripts via Spyder

While Jupyter notebook is a good place to start writing Python programs, once you get comfortable with Python, you should move to Spyder IDE. Spyder allows us to directly create Python files. Spyder is similar to more conventional text editors with options to Run file, Run piece of code, debug code etc.

Just like Jupyter notebook, you can run Spyder from Anaconda Navigator or directly from Start Menu. You will be presented with the following interface once you run Spyder.

On the left side of the Spyder interface, you can see text editor; this is where you enter your script. On the bottom right you have console window. You can directly execute scripts in the console window. Furthermore, the output of the code written in the editor also appears in the console window. Let's write hello world program in Spyder.

To run script in Python you have two options. You can either click the green triangle from the top menu or you can select the piece of code you want to execute and press CTRL + ENTER from the keyboard. You will see the output in the console window.

What's next?

In this chapter we saw the process of setting up the environment required to run python programs. We wrote our first python program in two different editors. In the next chapter we will start our discussion about data preprocessing for machine learning.

Chapter 3

Data Preprocessing For Machine Learning

Data has to be in a specific format before you can apply machine learning algorithms to them. Converting data to the right format for machine learning algorithms is usually known as data preprocessing. Depending upon the dataset, there are several preprocessing steps that are required to be performed to convert data into a format usable by machine learning algorithm. Following are the steps involved in preprocessing data for machine learning algorithms:

1- Getting the dataset
2- Import libraries
3- Import the dataset
4- Handling missing values
5- Handling categorical data

6- Dividing data into training and tests sets

7- Scaling the data

In this chapter we will study each of these steps in details.

Getting the Dataset

All the datasets that we are going to use in this book can be found at this link:

https://drive.google.com/file/d/1TB0tMuLv uL0Ad1dzHRyxBX9cseOhUs_4/view?usp=sh aring

Download the "rar" file, and copy the "Datasets" folder into your D drive. All the algorithms in the book access the datasets from "D:/Datasets" folder. The dataset that we are going to use in this first chapter for preprocessing is called "patients.csv".

If you go to your Datasets folder and open the patients.csv file with Microsoft Excel, it looks like this:

Age	BMI	Gender	Diabetic
25	25	Male	No
55	31	Female	Yes
40	28	Male	Yes
61	24	Male	No
24		Female	No
35	35	Male	Yes
52	32	Male	Yes
67	26	Female	No
44	27	Male	No
19	22	Female	No
58	89	Female	Yes
48	39	Male	Yes

The dataset contains information about Age, BMI (Body Mass Index) and Gender of 12 patients. The dataset also contains a column that shows whether patients are Diabetic or not. The Age and BMI columns are numeric since they contain numeric values while the Gender and Diabetic columns are categorical.

Another important distinction that you need to make before you use your dataset for machine learning is between independent and dependent variable. As a rule of thumb, the variable whose value is to be predicted is dependent variable and the variables that are used for making predictions are independent variables. For instance in the patients.csv dataset, Age, BMI and Gender variables are independent while the fourth column i.e. Diabetic is the dependent variable as its value is dependent on the first three columns.

Import Libraries

Python comes with a variety of prebuild libraries that perform different tasks. In this book we will be using Python's Scikit Learn Library. However for now we will only install three of the most essential libraries that we will need in almost every machine learning application. These libraries are *numpy*, *matplotlib.pyplot* and *pandas.*

numpy

The *numpy* library is used performs variety of advanced mathematical functions. Since machine learning algorithms make heavy use of mathematics, it is highly recommended that you install the *numpy* library.

matplotlib.pyplot

This library is used to plot beautiful charts. To get intuition about our data and results, we will need to this library.

pandas

Finally, the third library that we are going to install in this chapter is the *pandas* library. The *pandas* library is used to easily import and view the datasets.

To import these three libraries, create a new Python notebook in *Jupyter* or Open a new file in *Spyder* (The codes in this chapter are executed in *Spyder*) and execute the following lines of code.

```
import numpy as np
import matplotlib.pyplot as plt
```

```
import pandas as pd
```

To import a library in Python, keyword *import* is used. In the script above we import *numpy* as *np, matplotlib.pyplot* as *plt* and *pandas* as *pd*, respectively. Here *np, plt* and *pd* are nicknames. We will use these nicknames to call different functions of these libraries.

Import the Dataset

We have downloaded the libraries in last section. In this section, we will import the dataset into the application that we created in last section. You will also get to know why we imported the *pandas* library.

Our dataset is in CSV (Comma Separated Values) format. The *pandas* library contains *read_csv* function that takes the path to the CSV formatted dataset as parameter and loads the dataset into *pandas dataframe* which is basically an object that stores dataset in the form of columns and rows.

Execute the following script (below the script that loads the libraries) to load the patients.csv dataset to the application.

```
patient_data                    =
pd.read_csv("D:/Datasets/patients.cs
v")
```

The script above loads the patients.csv dataset in the Datasets folder of the D drive to **patients_data dataframe.**

If you are using *Jupyter* notebook, simply execute the following script to see how your data looks:

```
patient_data.head()
```

On the other hand, if you are using *Spyder*, go to Variable explorer and double click *patient_data* variable from the list of variables as shown below:

Once you click the *patient_data* variable, you will see the details of the patients.csv dataset as shown in the figure below:

You can see that a *pandas dataframe* looks like a matrix with zero based index.

Once we have loaded the dataset, the next step is to divide the dataset into a matrix of features and vector of dependent variables. Feature set consists of all the independent variables. For instance the feature matrix for the patients.csv dataset will contain Age, BMI and Gender columns. The size of the feature matrix is equal to the number of independent variables by the number of records. In this case the feature matrix will be of size 3 x 12 since there are three independent variable and 12 records.

Let's first create a feature features. You can give any name to the feature matrix but conventionally in machine learning community, feature matrix is denoted by capital X. However for the sake of readability we will name it *features* Execute the following script:

```
features=
patient_data.iloc[:,0:3].value
s
```

In the script above we use the *iloc* function of the *dataframe* to select all the rows and the first three columns from the *patient_data* dataframe. The iloc function takes two parameters. The first is the range of rows to select and the second is the range of columns to select. We only specified colon as first parameter which means that filter all the rows from the dataset. In the second parameter after the comma we specified a range of columns i.e. column 0 to 3. This returns columns 0, 1 and 2. Remember the *iloc* returns one less than the upper range of column. The 0, 1 and 2 columns mean Age, BMI and Gender since python follows zero based index. Therefore Age is considered 0th column.

If now you print the features in the console window, you will see following result:

```
array([[25, 25.0, 'Male'],
       [55, 31.0, 'Female'],
       [40, 28.0, 'Male'],
       [61, 24.0, 'Male'],
       [24, nan, 'Female'],
       [35, 35.0, 'Male'],
       [52, 32.0, 'Male'],
       [67, 26.0, 'Female'],
       [44, 27.0, 'Male'],
       [19, 22.0, 'Female'],
       [58, 89.0, 'Female'],
       [48, 39.0, 'Male']], dtype=object)
```

You can see it is a two dimensional array of feature set.

Similarly, to create a label vector, execute the following script:

```
labels=
patient_data.iloc[:,3].values
```

Now we have our feature matrix as well as label vector. The next step is to handle the missing values (if any) in the dataset.

Handling Missing Values

If you look at the patient_data object you will see that the record at index 4 has missing value for BMI column. To handle missing values, the simplest approach is to remove the record with missing values. However, sometimes a record contains crucial information and should not be removed just because one column has a missing value.

Another approach to deal with missing values is to replace missing value with some value. Missing values can be replaced by mean or median of all the values in the column.

To handle the missing values we will use the *Imputer* class of the *sklearn.preprocessing* library. Take a look at the following script.

```
from     sklearn.preprocessing
import Imputer
imputer               =
Imputer(missing_values="NaN",
strategy="mean", axis=0)
imputer               =
imputer.fit(features[:,1:2])
features[:,1:2]       =
imputer.transform(features[:,1
:2])
```

In the script above, the first line imports the *Imputer* class from *sklearn.preprocessing* library. Next we create object of the Imputer class. Imputer class constructor takes three parameters: *missing_value*, *strategy* and *axis*. The missing_value parameter specifies the value that is required to be replaced. In our dataset, missing values have been denoted by "nan", therefore we specified "NaN" for *missing_value* parameter. Strategy parameter specifies the type of strategy we want to use to fill missing value, it can have *mean, median*, and *most_frequent* values. Finally, the *axis* parameter denotes the axis along which we want to imputate. The *axis 0* specifies the column axis whereas *axis 1* specifies the row axis.

Next we execute *fit* method of the Imputer class. This method takes the column that we want to handle missing values for, as input. Finally we execute *transform* function which actually fills missing values in column 1 by the mean of the column. When you execute the script above you will see that that the record at index 4 that previously had missing value for column1 i.e. BMI, now contains the mean of all the values in the BMI column. This is shown in the following screenshot:

```
array([[25, 25.0, 'Male'],
       [55, 31.0, 'Female'],
       [40, 28.0, 'Male'],
       [61, 24.0, 'Male'],
       [24, 34.36363636363637, 'Female'],
       [35, 35.0, 'Male'],
       [52, 32.0, 'Male'],
       [67, 26.0, 'Female'],
       [44, 27.0, 'Male'],
       [19, 22.0, 'Female'],
       [58, 89.0, 'Female'],
       [48, 39.0, 'Male']], dtype=object)
```

Handling Categorical Data

We know machine learning algorithms are based on mathematical concepts and mathematics is all about numbers. Therefore, it is convenient to convert all the categorical values in our dataset to numeric values. If we look at the patients.csv we have two columns with categorical values: Gender and Diabetic.

Luckily, in sklearn.preprocessing library we have LabelEncoder class which takes categorical column as input and returns corresponding numerical output. Take a look at the following script:

```
from      sklearn.preprocessing
import LabelEncoder
labelencoder_features        =
LabelEncoder()
features[:,2]=
labelencoder_features.fit_tran
sform(features[:,2])
```

Like Imputer class, *LabelEncoder* class has *fit_transform* method, which is basically a combination of *fit* and *transform* methods. The class takes categorical column as input and returns corresponding numeric values. In the script above we pass it Gender column i.e. the column at index 2 to the *LabelEncoder* class. After executing the script above if you check the values of Gender column, you will see ones and zeros in place of Male and Female as shown below:

```
array([[25, 25.0, 1],
       [55, 31.0, 0],
       [40, 28.0, 1],
       [61, 24.0, 1],
       [24, 34.36363636363637, 0],
       [35, 35.0, 1],
       [52, 32.0, 1],
       [67, 26.0, 0],
       [44, 27.0, 1],
       [19, 22.0, 0],
       [58, 89.0, 0],
       [48, 39.0, 1]], dtype=object)
```

Similarly, the labels vector can also be converted into set of numeric values as follows:

```
labels                    =
labelencoder_features.fit_tran
sform(labels)
```

Dividing data into training and tests sets

In the first chapter we discussed that machine learning models are trained on subset of dataset and tested on another subset of the dataset. This splitting between the training and test set is done to ensure that our machine learning algorithm doesn't *overfit*. *Overfitting* refers to the phenomena where machine learning performs excellent results on training data but poor results on test data. A good machine learning model is the one that gives good result on both training and test data. That way we can say that our model has correctly learned the underlying assumptions from the dataset and can be used to correctly make decisions on any new dataset.

The *sklearn.model_selection* library contains *train_test_split* class that can be used to divide data into train and test sets. The class accepts features, labels and *test_size* as parameters. The *test_size* defines the size of the test set. Test size of 0.5 means split the data into 50% of test size and 50% of training size. The following script divides the data into 75% train size and 25% test size.

```
from   sklearn.model_selection
import train_test_split
```

```
train_features, test_features,
train_labels, test_labels =
train_test_split(features,
labels, test_size = 0.25,
random_state = 0)
```

When you execute the above script you will see that *train_features* variable will contain matrix of 9 features (75% of 12) while *train_labels* will contain corresponding 9 labels. Similarly *test_features* will contain a matrix of 3 features (25% of 12) while *test_labels* will contain corresponding 3 labels.

Scaling the Data

The final preprocessing step before we can feed our data to machine learning algorithm is that of feature scaling. We need to scale features because in some datasets there is a huge difference between the values of different features. For instance if we add number of red blood cells of patients out patients.csv dataset, the column will have values in hundreds of thousands, on the other hand the Age column can have very small values. Many of the machines learning models use Euclidean distance to find distance between data points. If features are not scaled, these algorithms can be biased towards features with large values.

There are two ways to scale features:

Standardization: $\dfrac{x - mean(x)}{standard\,deviation(x)}$

And

Normalization: $\dfrac{x - min(x)}{\max(x) - \min(x)}$

The *sklearn.preprocessing* library contains *StandardScaler* class that can be used to implement standardization of features. Like other preprocessing classes, it contains *fit_transform* method that takes dataset as input and returns scaled dataset. The following script scales both the *train_features* and *test_features* datasets.

```
from     sklearn.preprocessing
import StandardScaler
```

```
feature_scaler                =
StandardScaler()
train_features                =
feature_scaler.fit_transform(t
rain_features)
test_features                 =
feature_scaler.transform(test_
features)
```

Now if you see *train_features* and *test_features,* you can see scaled values as shown below:

```
In [15]: train_features
Out[15]:
array([[ 0.83652186,  2.77984695, -1.11803399],
       [-0.31192341, -0.30949713,  0.89442719],
       [-0.05671335, -0.36014212,  0.89442719],
       [ 0.64511432, -0.15756218, -1.11803399],
       [ 1.41074449, -0.4107871 , -1.11803399],
       [-1.65177621, -0.61336704, -1.11803399],
       [ 1.0279294 , -0.51207707,  0.89442719],
       [-1.26896113, -0.46143209,  0.89442719],
       [-0.63093598,  0.04501776,  0.89442719]])

In [16]: test_features
Out[16]:
array([[ 0.45370677, -0.10691719,  0.89442719],
       [ 0.19849671,  0.2475977 ,  0.89442719],
       [-1.33276364,  0.01278914, -1.11803399]])
```

There is no need to scale labels for classification problems. For regression

278

problems we will see how to scale labels in regression section.

Conclusion

In this chapter we saw how we can preprocess data before using it for actual machine learning tasks. In the next chapter we will start new section i.e. Regression. The first machine learning algorithm that we will study will be linear regression.

Chapter 4

Linear Regression

In this chapter we will start our discussion with the first supervised machine learning algorithm i.e. Linear Regression which is a type of regression algorithm. In this chapter we will study linear regression with one variable as well as linear regression with multiple variables. Using linear regression with one variable, we will predict price of a car based on the year of manufacture. We will then move to more complex problem where we will predict the points that a basketball player can score based on height, weight, field goals and throws. However, first let's study theoretical back ground of linear regression.

Theory of Linear Regression

In simple words, linear regression is an approach that identifies relationship between two or more than two variables. Mathematical, linear regression finds a linear function that maps independent variables to dependent variables. If this function is plotted on 2-D space, it results in a straight line.

Consider a scenario where we want to find relationship between the price of cars and the year of manufacture. If we plot the year on x-axis and price on y-axis, linear regression algorithm will find a straight line that best fits the data points. This is shown in the figure below:

We know that straight line can be represented as:

$$b = ax1 + c$$

Here b is the dependent variable, *a* is the slope of the line, *x* is the independent variable and c is the y intercept.

If we look at the equation we can see that b and x remain constant since they are the data variables. Therefore, linear regression algorithm gives us the slope and the intercept that best result in line which best fits the dataset.

This concept can be extended to more than one independent variable. The equation for linear regression function will then be represented as:

$$b = a1x1 + a2x2 + a3x3 + \ldots\ldots anxn + c$$

Here is n is the total number of independent variables. This equation basically represents a hyper plane with n-dimension. It is important to mention that in two-dimensions linear regression model can be represented as a straight line. In three dimensions, it is represented in the form of plane and in more than three dimensions; it is represented as hyper plane.

Enough of the theory, let's implement linear regression with the help of Python's Scikit learn library.

Linear Regression with One Variable

For the sake of simplicity, we will first implement linear regression with one variable. It is also known as Univariate Linear

Regression. In this case, there is only one independent and one dependent variable.

In this section we will use the "*car_price.csv*" to predict the price of car (dependent variable) based on the year of manufacture (independent variable). You can find the dataset in the supplementary "Datasets" folder.

To predict the price, we will use linear regression algorithm implemented via Python Scikit Learn Library. So, let the fun begin:

1- Importing Required Libraries

As discussed in the previous chapter, the first step in implementing any machine learning algorithm is to import required libraries into your program. The following code imports required libraries:

```
import pandas as pd
import numpy as np
import matplotlib.pyplot as plt
```

```
%matplotlib inline
```

This script is implemented using Jupyter notebook. Therefore, to draw graphs within the notebook, we have used the command %matplotlib inline. If you are using Spyder, you can remove the last line.

2- Importing the Dataset

Once you imported the libraries, the next step is to import the dataset that you are going to use for training the algorithm. We will be using "car_price.csv" dataset. Execute the following script to import the dataset:

```
car_data =
pd.read_csv('D:\Datasets\car_p
rice.csv')
```

The script above reads the dataset and stores it in *car_data dataframe*.

3- Analyzing the Data

Before using the data for training, it is always a good practice to analyze your data for any missing values or scaling.

Let's first take a general look of our data. The *head* function returns the first 5 rows of the dataset. Execute the following script:

```
car_data.head()
```

	Year	Price
0	1980	2000
1	1985	3000
2	1983	2200
3	1990	3700
4	1995	4500

Similarly, the describe function returns all the statistical details of the dataset.

```
car_data.describe()
```

	Year	Price
count	20.000000	20.000000
mean	1992.100000	4302.500000
std	7.319045	1458.592959
min	1980.000000	2000.000000
25%	1986.500000	3075.000000
50%	1992.500000	4350.000000
75%	1998.250000	5325.000000
max	2005.000000	7000.000000

Finally let us see if linear regression algorithm is actually suitable for this task. Let's plot our data points on the graph and see if we can see some sort of linear relation between price and year. Execute the following script:

```
plt.scatter(car_data['Year'],
car_data['Price'])
plt.title("Year vs Price")
plt.xlabel("Year")
plt.ylabel("Price")
plt.show()
```

The output of the script above looks like this:

In the script above, we use the scatter plot from the *matplotlib* library to plot year on x and price on y axis. From the output figure we can clearly see that with the increase in year number the price of car increase.
There is a linear relationship between the year and price. Therefore, we can use linear regression algorithm to solve this problem.

4- Data Preprocessing

In the last chapter, we studied that before we feed the data to learning algorithms, we first have to divide the data into feature and label set and then test and training set. In this step we will perform these two tasks.

To divide the data into features and labels, execute the following script:

```
features=
car_data.iloc[:,0:1].values
labels=
car_data.iloc[:,1].values
```

Since we have only two columns, the 0th column contains the feature set while the 1st column contains the labels.

Finally let's divide the data into 80 % training and 20% test sets:

```
from sklearn.model_selection
import train_test_split

train_features, test_features,
train_labels, test_labels =
train_test_split(features,
labels, test_size = 0.2,
random_state = 0)
```

If we look at the dataset we can see that there is not a very huge difference between values of years and prices. Both of them have in thousands. Therefore, there is no need to scale the data and we can use this data as it is for training the algorithm.

5- Training the Algorithm and making Predictions

The *LinearRegression* class of the *sklearn.linear_model* is used to implement linear regression in Python. The LinearRegression class has fit method that takes training features and labels as input and train the model as shown below:

```
from sklearn.linear_model
import LinearRegression
lin_reg = LinearRegression()
lin_reg.fit(train_features,
train_labels)
```

Let's see what the coefficient is found by our model for the only independent variable. Execute the following script:

```
print(lin_reg.coef_)
```

The result will be: 204.815

This shows that for a unit change in year, the value of Car price increases by 204.815

Once the model is trained the final step is to predict the out of the new instance. The *predict* method of the *LinearRegression* class can be used for this purpose. The method takes test features as input and predicts the corresponding labels as output.

Execute the following script to predict the label for the test features:

```
predictions = lin_reg.predict(
test_features)
```

All the predictions are stored in the *predictions* variable.

Let's compare the predicted value with the actual values. Execute the following script to do so:

```
comparison=pd.DataFrame({'Real
':test_labels,
'Predictions':predictions})
```

```
print(comparison)
```

The output looks like this:

```
   Predictions   Real
0  5689.172831   5200
1  2821.751476   3000
2  2616.935665   3100
3  3641.014720   4000
```

We can see that there are four values in the test set which is 20% of the whole dataset as specified in the *train_test_split.* You can see our values are close but not exact.

To evaluate performance of a machine learning model, three metrics are commonly used: Mean Absolute Error (MAE), Mean Squared Error (MSE) and Root Mean Squared Error (RMSE). Luckily we don't have to code the complex mathematics behind these metrics. The metrics class of the *sklearn* library contains functions that can be used to find values for these metrics. Execute the following script to find MAE, MSE and RMSE for our linear regression model.

```
from sklearn import metrics
print('MAE:',
metrics.mean_absolute_error(te
st_labels, predictions))
print('MSE:',
metrics.mean_squared_error(tes
t_labels, predictions))
print('RMSE:',
np.sqrt(metrics.mean_squared_e
rror(test_labels,
predictions)))
```

The output is always follows:

```
MAE: 377.367742659
MSE: 158321.044602
RMSE: 397.895771028
```

Normally if the value of MAE and RMSE is less than 10% of the mean value for the predicted column, the algorithm performance is considered a good. However lesser the values of MAE and RMSE, higher will be the performance of the algorithm. In our case the values of MAE and RMSE are 377.36 and 397.85 which is lesser than 10%

of the mean value of Price which is 430.2. Hence we can say that our algorithm performance is good.

Linear Regression with Multiple Variables

Linear regression with multiple variable or multivariate linear regression involves more than one independent variables. In this section we will use Python's *Scikit* Learn library to implement Multivariate linear regression.

We will predict how much points can a player score in a basketball match based on his height, weight, percentage of successful field goals out of all attempts, percentage of successful throws out of all attempts. We have downloaded the dataset and it is available in the Datasets folder. The dataset can also be downloaded from this link:

http://college.cengage.com/mathematics/b rase/understandable_statistics/7e/students /datasets/mlr/frames/frame.html

We will follow almost same steps for this problem that we followed for single variable linear regression. We will start with importing libraries and dataset, followed by data analysis and preprocessing. Finally we will train our linear regression algorithm and will evaluate its performance.

1- Importing Required Libraries

The following code imports required libraries:

```
import pandas as pd
import numpy as np
import matplotlib.pyplot as plt
%matplotlib inline
```

2- Importing the Dataset

Though the dataset is available online, we have downloaded it an added it in the dataset repository available with this book. The dataset name is "player.csv'. Execute the following command to import the dataset.

```
player_data =
pd.read_csv('D:\Datasets\playe
r.csv')
```

The script above reads the dataset and stores it in *player_data dataframe*.

3- Analyzing the Data

Execute the following script to eyeball the data:

```
player_data.head()
```

The output looks like this:

	Height	Weight	Field_Goals	Throws	Points
0	6.8	225	0.442	0.672	9.2
1	6.3	180	0.435	0.797	11.7
2	6.4	190	0.456	0.761	15.8
3	6.2	180	0.416	0.651	8.6
4	6.9	205	0.449	0.900	23.2

Execute the following script to get the statistical details of the

```
player_data.describe()
```

	Height	Weight	Field_Goals	Throws	Points
count	54.000000	54.000000	54.000000	54.000000	54.000000
mean	6.587037	209.907407	0.449111	0.741852	11.790741
std	0.458894	30.265036	0.056551	0.100146	5.899257
min	5.700000	105.000000	0.291000	0.244000	2.800000
25%	6.225000	185.000000	0.415250	0.713000	8.150000
50%	6.650000	212.500000	0.443500	0.753500	10.750000
75%	6.900000	235.000000	0.483500	0.795250	13.600000
max	7.600000	263.000000	0.599000	0.900000	27.400000

4- Data Preprocessing

To following script divides the data into feature and label set.

```
features =
player_data[['Height','Weight'
,'Field_Goals','Throws']]
labels = player_data['Points']
```

It is important to mention that in addition to using iloc function of the dataframe, you can also divide the data into feature and label set by specifying the name of the columns as shown in the above script.

Finally let's divide the data into 80 % training and 20% test sets:

```
from sklearn.model_selection
import train_test_split

train_features, test_features,
train_labels, test_labels =
train_test_split(features,
labels, test_size = 0.2,
random_state = 0)
```

5- Scaling the Data

If look at the dataset it is not scaled well, for instance the *Field_Goals* and *Throws* column have values between 0 and 1, while the rest of the columns have higher values. Therefore, before training the algorithm, we will scale our data down. Remember we discussed scaling in the last chapter. Here we will use the standard scalar class.

```
from sklearn.preprocessing
import StandardScaler

feature_scaler =
StandardScaler()

train_features =
feature_scaler.fit_transform(t
rain_features)
```

```
test_features =
feature_scaler.transform(test_
features)
```

6- Training the Algorithm and making Predictions

For multivariate linear regression, we will again use the same *LinearRegression* class of the *sklearn.linear_model* library. Execute the following script to train the model

```
from sklearn.linear_model
import LinearRegression

lin_reg = LinearRegression()

lin_reg.fit(train_features,
train_labels)
```

Let's see what the coefficient is found by our model for the only independent variable. Execute the following script:

```
coefficients=
pd.DataFrame(lin_reg.coef_,fea
tures.columns,columns=['Coeffi
cients'])
```

```
print(coefficients)
```

The output looks like this:

```
               Coefficients
  Height          -2.582632
  Weight           1.294067
  Field_Goals      2.879289
  Throws           1.035310
```

The output shows that for unit increase in
Height, there is a decrease of 2.58 percent in
the point scored by the player. Similarly for
unit increase in weight, the number of points
scored increase by 1.29 and so on.

This shows that for a unit change in year, the
value of Car price increases by 204.815

Once the model is trained the final step is to
predict the out of the new instance. The
predict method of the *LinearRegression* class
can be used for this purpose.

Execute the following script to predict the
label for the test features:

```
predictions = lin_reg.predict(
test_features)
```

To compare predictions with real outputs, execute the following script:

Let's compare the predicted value with the actual values. Execute the following script to do so:

```
comparison=pd.DataFrame({'Real
':test_labels,
'Predictions':predictions})
print(comparison)
```

The output looks like this:

```
      Predictions   Real
53      10.342831    8.3
33      11.431936    7.2
48       9.637807    2.8
26      14.690648    5.6
11      14.363039    9.1
2       12.763432   15.8
32      14.397398    9.6
42      14.473602   15.4
45       7.550197    7.9
30      14.867451   11.7
4       11.721830   23.2
```

From the output, you can see that the predicted values are not really close to the actual values.

Execute the following script to find MAE, MSE and RMSE for our linear regression model.

```
from sklearn import metrics
print('MAE:',
metrics.mean_absolute_error(te
st_labels, predictions))
print('MSE:',
metrics.mean_squared_error(tes
t_labels, predictions))
print('RMSE:',
np.sqrt(metrics.mean_squared_e
rror(test_labels,
predictions)))
```

The output is always follows:

```
MAE: 4.65654985924
MSE: 32.1977246142
RMSE: 5.67430388808
```

RMSE are 4.65 and 5.67 which is greater than 10% of the mean value of point which is 1.179 Hence, we can say that our algorithm is not performing good on this dataset. There are many reasons why an algorithm can perform poorly and how to improve the performance and algorithm which we will discuss in a later chapter.

Conclusion

In this chapter, we studied our first supervised algorithm i.e. linear regression. We saw what univariate and multivariate linear regressions are and how they can be implemented via Python Scikit learn library. In the next chapter, we will study Polynomial Regression which is basically non-linear regression.

Chapter 5

Polynomial Regression

In the last chapter we studied how linear regression algorithm can be used to find the straight line that best fits the data points. However, in real world, data is not always linearly related. For instance if you take a look at the data distribution in the following figure

Here if we draw a straight line that best fits the data points, some points will end up above the line the other would end up below the line as shown in the following figure. In such a case, the chance of error in prediction will be higher.

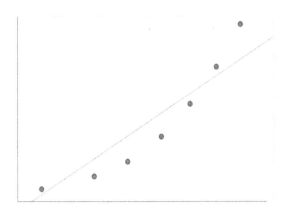

On the other hand if we have a curved line that fits all the data points as shown in the following figure, the chance of error can be minimized.

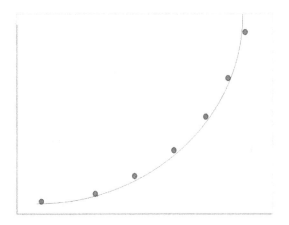

In polynomial regression we try to find models that are not straight lines but they fit the data points more accurately.

In the last chapter we discussed that the straight linear model can be represented as:

B= a1x1+ a2x2+a3x3 + ……………….
Anxn

On the other hand, polynomial regression results in a mode of degree greater than 1 e.g

$$B= a1x1^2 + a2x2^3 +a3x3^2 + ……………….$$
$$Anxn^5$$

Polynomial Regression with Python Scikit Learn

Let's implement polynomial regression with Python Scikit Learn. The problem that we are going to solve in this section is to predict the consumption of gas(in millions) in the 48 states of US based on features such as paved highways (miles), petrol tax (cents), per capita income, and ratio of individuals with driving license.

For further details of the dataset, visit this link. The data can be downloaded from the link as well, however the data is not in CSV format at the download link. For the ease of the readers, the data has been downloaded, converted to CSV and saved in the Datasets folder with name "petrol_data.csv" you can found it there.

As always, the first step is to import the required libraries:

1- Importing Required Libraries

The following code imports required libraries:

```
import pandas as pd
import numpy as np
import matplotlib.pyplot as plt
```

```
%matplotlib inline
```

This script is implemented using Jupyter notebook. Therefore, to draw graphs within the notebook, we have used the command %matplotlib inline. If you are using Spyder, you can remove the last line.

2- Importing the Dataset

Execute the following command to import the dataset.

```
petrol_data =
pd.read_csv('D:\Datasets\petro
l_data.csv')
```

The script above reads the dataset and stores it in *player_data dataframe*.

3- Analyzing the Data

Execute the following script to eyeball the data:

```
petrol_data.head()
```

The output looks like this:

	Petrol_tax	Average_income	Paved_Highways	Population_Driver_licence(%)	Petrol_Consumption
0	9.0	3571	1976	0.525	541
1	9.0	4092	1250	0.572	524
2	9.0	3865	1586	0.580	561
3	7.5	4870	2351	0.529	414
4	8.0	4399	431	0.544	410

Execute the following script to get the statistical details of the

```
petrol_data.describe()
```

	Petrol_tax	Average_income	Paved_Highways	Population_Driver_licence(%)	Petrol_Consumption
count	48.000000	48.000000	48.000000	48.000000	48.000000
mean	7.668333	4241.833333	5565.416667	0.570333	576.770833
std	0.950770	573.623768	3491.507166	0.055470	111.885816
min	5.000000	3063.000000	431.000000	0.451000	344.000000
25%	7.000000	3739.000000	3110.250000	0.529750	509.500000
50%	7.500000	4298.000000	4735.500000	0.564500	568.500000
75%	8.125000	4578.750000	7156.000000	0.595250	632.750000
max	10.000000	5342.000000	17782.000000	0.724000	968.000000

4- Data Preprocessing

To following script divides the data into feature and label set.

```
features =
player_data[['Height','Weight'
,'Field_Goals','Throws']]
labels = player_data['Points']
```

Finally let's divide the data into 80 % training and 20% test sets:

```
from sklearn.model_selection
import train_test_split
```

```
train_features, test_features,
train_labels, test_labels =
train_test_split(features,
labels, test_size = 0.2,
random_state = 0)
```

5- Generating Polynomial Features

To implement Polynomial Regression using Python's Scikit Learn library, the same LinearRegression class is used. However before feeding our data to the algorithm, we need to convert linear features into polynomial features i.e. feature with higher degrees. If you look at the feature set we have 4 features at the moment. If we convert these linear features to polynomial features of degree 2, we will end up with 15 features. Three features for each column, i.e. feature with degree 0, 1 and 2. We have 4 features, therefore 4 x 3 = 12. In addition we also have cross terms in polynomial regression. We have four features, therefore we will have three cross terms i.e. column1 x column2, column2 x column3 and column3xcolumn4.

Let's see how we can convert linear features to polynomial features with Python Scikit learn library. Execute the following script:

```
from sklearn.preprocessing
import PolynomialFeatures

poly_reg_feat =
PolynomialFeatures(degree=2)

train_features_poly =
poly_reg_feat.fit_transform(tr
ain_features)

test_features_poly =
poly_reg_feat.transform(test_f
eatures)
```

Take a careful look at the script above. To implement polynomial regression the *PolynomialFeature* class from the *sklearn.preprocessing* library is used. Degree of polynomial is passed to the class constructor. Next the *fit_transform* method is called and the original feature set is passed to this method. The *fit_transform* method returns polynomial feature set. Now if you check the columns of *train_feature_poly* and *test_features_poly* variables, you will see that they will contain 15 columns, instead of the original four.

6- Scaling the Data

It is always a good practice to scale your data in case of polynomial regression since the degree of the features is different which can result in highly un-scaled data. Therefore, before training the algorithm, we will scale our data down. Here we will use the standard scalar class.

```
from sklearn.preprocessing
import StandardScaler

feature_scaler =
StandardScaler()

train_features_poly =
feature_scaler.fit_transform(t
rain_features_poly)

test_features_poly =
feature_scaler.transform(test_
features_poly)
```

7- Training the Algorithm and making Predictions

As earlier said, for polynomial regression, we will again use the same *LinearRegression* class of the *sklearn.linear_model* library. Execute the following script to train the model

```
from sklearn.linear_model
import LinearRegression

lin_reg = LinearRegression()

lin_reg.fit(train_features_pol
y, train_labels)
```

Similarly, to make predictions,

Execute the following script:

```
predictions =
lin_reg.predict(test_features_
poly)
```

Let's compare the predicted value with the actual values. Execute the following script to do so:

```
comparison=pd.DataFrame({'Real
':test_labels,
'Predictions':predictions})
print(comparison)
```

The output looks like this:

```
    Predictions   Real
0   553.577485    534
1   547.261229    410
2   577.220482    577
3   580.830717    571
4   558.903290    577
5   639.422694    704
6   568.688917    487
7   677.972568    587
8   401.726005    467
9   500.578904    580
```

From the output, it can be seen that if not accurate, our algorithm is still making some pretty close predictions.

8- Evaluating the Algorithm

As always, the last step of any machine learning process is to evaluate performance of the trained algorithm. As discussed earlier, for regression the performance is evaluated in terms of mean absolute error, mean squared error and root mean squared error. The following script finds these values for our algorithm:

```
from sklearn import metrics
print('MAE:',
metrics.mean_absolute_error(te
st_labels, predictions))
print('MSE:',
metrics.mean_squared_error(tes
t_labels, predictions))
print('RMSE:',
np.sqrt(metrics.mean_squared_e
rror(test_labels,
predictions)))
```

The output values are as follows:

```
MAE: 56.6920504483
MSE: 4933.58260557
RMSE: 70.2394661538
```

The value of MAE is 56.69 which is less than 10% of the mean value of petrol consumption 57.67. However for RMSE the value is 70.23 which means that our dataset has outliers which needs to be dealt with. Overall, the performance of our algorithm is good.

Conclusion

In this chapter we studied Polynomial regression which is a type of supervised regression algorithm. In the next chapter, we will see how decision tree algorithm can be used for regression purposes.

Chapter 6

Decision Tree for Regression

In the last two chapters we studied Linear Regression and Polynomial Regression algorithms. These algorithms are based on the principle of error correction using gradient decent algorithm. In this chapter we are going to study another extremely powerful machine learning algorithm based on entropy.

The principle behind the working of a decision tree is very simple. Each feature in the dataset is treated as a node in the decision tree. At each node a decision is made regarding which path to choose in the tree depending upon the value of the feature at that particular node. The process continues until the leaf node is reached. Leaf node contains the final decision.

This explanation might seem daunting at first but we have been using decision trees all our life. Suppose there is a bank that has to decide whether loan should be given to a particular customer or not. The bank has customer data including age, gender and salary. Bank has to decide whether the customer should be give loan or not.

A bank may define criteria which consists of set of rules that defines whether the loan will be awarded or not. These rules can look like this.

1. If the age of the customer is greater than 25 and less than 60, then go to next step. Else simply reject the loan application.
2. If the first condition is satisfied, then check if the person is salaried or not. If the person is salaried, go to step 3 else if the person is jobless, reject the loan application.

3. If the person is salaried and gender is male, go to step 4. Else if the gender is female go to step 5.
4. If the salary is greater than 35000 dollars per year, award the loan else reject the application.
5. If the salary is greater than 45000 dollars per year, award the loan else reject the application.

The decision tree based on such rules looks like this:

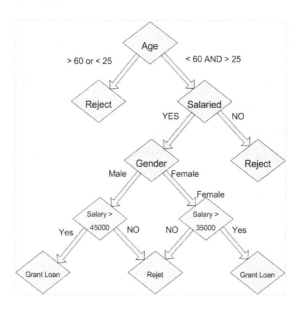

The above set of rules is very simplistic and is chosen randomly. In real world the data is much more complex and statistical techniques such as entropy are used to create these nodes. Entropy refers to the impurity of classification in the labeled data. Basically in decision trees, the feature that results in minimum entropy in the output labels is set at root node. For instance, if 95% of the times when the age is greater than 60 and less than 25, the application for loan is rejected, the impurity in the output will be 5% for Age with values between 60 and 25. Similarly, if in 80 of the cases the loan for jobless person is rejected, the impurity in the output label for salaried attribute will be 20%. As a rule of thumb, the features with lesser impurity are placed higher in the tree nodes.

Benefits of Decision Trees

Decision trees can be very handy because of their simplicity and ease of understanding.

Following are some of the advantages of decision tree algorithm.

1- Decision trees work equally well for regression as well as classification tasks which means that you can predict continuous as well as discrete values.
2- Decision trees can be used to classify linear as well as non-linear data.
3- In comparison to most of the other machine learning algorithms, they are relatively faster to train.

Using Python Scikit Learn Library to Implement Decision Trees

As always, we will use Python's Scikit Learn Library to see decision trees in action. In this section we will again predict the consumption of petrol (in millions) in the 48 states of US based on features such as paved highways (miles), petrol tax (cents), per capita income, and ratio of individuals with driving license.

For further details of the dataset, visit this link. The data can be downloaded from the link as well; however the data is not in CSV format at the download link. For the ease of the readers, the data has been downloaded, converted to CSV and saved in the Datasets folder with name "petrol_data.csv" you can found it there.

Now you should be familiar with the machine learning process. The first step to solve every machine learning problem with Python is to import the required libraries. The following script does that:

1. Importing Necessary Libraries

```
import pandas as pd
import numpy as np
import matplotlib.pyplot as plt
%matplotlib inline
```

This script is implemented using Jupyter notebook. Therefore, to draw graphs within the notebook, we have used the command %matplotlib inline. If you are using Spyder, you can remove the last line.

2. Importing Dataset

Execute the following command to import the dataset.

```
petrol_data =
pd.read_csv('D:\Datasets\petro
l_data.csv')
```

The script above reads the dataset and stores it in *player_data dataframe*.

3. Data Analysis

Execute the following script to eyeball the data:

```
petrol_data.head()
```

The result looks like this:

	Petrol_tax	Average_income	Paved_Highways	Population_Driver_licence(%)	Petrol_Consumption
0	9.0	3571	1976	0.525	541
1	9.0	4092	1250	0.572	524
2	9.0	3865	1586	0.580	561
3	7.5	4870	2351	0.529	414
4	8.0	4399	431	0.544	410

4. Data Preprocessing

To following script divides the data into feature and label set.

```
features=
petrol_data.iloc[:,0:4].values
labels=
petrol_data.iloc[:,4].values
```

Finally let's divide the data into 80 % training and 20% test sets:

```
from sklearn.model_selection
import train_test_split

train_features, test_features,
train_labels, test_labels =
train_test_split(features,
labels, test_size = 0.2,
random_state = 0)
```

5. Data Scaling

If you look at the dataset, you can see that our data is not very well scaled. For instance, the feature *Population_Driver_License* has values between 0 and 1 while

Average_Income and Paved_Highways has values in thousand. Therefore, before feeding our data to the algorithm, we need to scale our features. Execute the following script to do so:

```
from sklearn.preprocessing
import StandardScaler
feature_scaler =
StandardScaler()
train_features_poly =
feature_scaler.fit_transform(t
rain_features)
test_features_poly =
feature_scaler.transform(test_
features)
```

6. Training the Algorithm

We have scaled our features down. Now is the time to train our algorithm. To implement decision tree for classification, we use the *DecisionTreeClassifier* class of the *sklearn.tree* library. The fit method of the class is used to train the algorithm. The training features and labels are passed to this fit as shown in the following script:

```
from sklearn.tree import
DecisionTreeClassifier

dt_reg =
DecisionTreeClassifier()

dt_reg.fit(train_features,
train_labels)
```

7. Make Predictions

Finally to make predictions we will use the predict method of the DecisionTreeClassifier class object dt_reg that we created in the last section. Test features will be passed to it as a parameter.

```
predictions =
dt_reg.predict(test_features)
```

Let's compare the predicted values with the actual values, execute the following script:

```
comparison=pd.DataFrame({'Real
':test_labels,
'Predictions':predictions})

print(comparison)
```

The output of the script above looks like this:

```
     Predictions  Real
0            591   534
1            714   410
2            566   577
3            547   571
4            566   577
5            566   704
6            591   487
7            610   587
8            460   467
9            464   580
```

8. Evaluating the Algorithm

The following script finds these values of mean absolute error, mean squared error and root mean squared error

```
from sklearn import metrics
print('MAE:',
metrics.mean_absolute_error(te
st_labels, predictions))
```

```
print('MSE:',
metrics.mean_squared_error(tes
t_labels, predictions))
print('RMSE:',
np.sqrt(metrics.mean_squared_e
rror(test_labels,
predictions)))
```

The output values are as follows:

```
MAE: 79.5
MSE: 14037.7
RMSE: 118.480800132
```

The value of MAE is 79, which is greater than MAE value calculated for Polynomial Regression algorithm in the last chapter. Similarly, the value of RMSE in the case of decision tree is 118 which is far greater than the value obtained using polynomial regression algorithm in the last chapter. Hence we can say that for predicting petrol prices given the dataset used in this chapter, Polynomial regression algorithm outperforms the Decision tree algorithm.

Conclusion

In this chapter we studied what decision tree algorithm is and how it can be used for regression. In the next chapter we will study Random Forest algorithm which is basically based on decision tree algorithm.

Chapter 7

Random Forest for Regression

In the last chapter we studied decision trees. A single decision tree can be biased depending upon the data. A better approach could be to use multiple decision trees that make their own prediction and then final prediction can be calculating by finding the average of all predictions made by all the trees. This approach is known as ensemble learning. In ensemble learning multiple algorithms of same or different types are joined together to create a more power machine learning model. Random forest is a type of ensemble learning models and can be used for supervised machine learning.

Random forest algorithm unites multiple decision tree algorithms, creating a forest. Therefore, the algorithm is called "Random Forest" algorithm. Like decision tree algorithm, random forest algorithm can be used to predict continuous values (regression) as well as discrete values (classification). In this article we will implement random forest algorithm with the help of Python's Scikit learn library for regression purpose. We will see how we can use random forest algorithm for Classification in the Classification section of the book.

Working of Random Forest Algorithm

Random forest algorithm performs following steps:

1. Choose K random data points from the dataset
2. Create a decision tree regression or classification algorithm based on the K data points.
3. Select the number of trees for random forest algorithm and perform steps 1 and 2 on each tree.
4. If the problem is regression, each tree predicts a continuous value; the final output can be calculated by taking mean of the values predicted by all the trees. If the problem at hand is classification problem, each tree predicts a discrete value. Final category can be selected by majority voting.

Pros of Random Forest Algorithm

There are several advantages of random forest algorithm, some of which have been enlisted below:

1. A random forest algorithm is one of the most stable algorithm and scales very well. Since there are multiple trees in the forest, introduction or removal of data from the dataset can impact a small portion of trees but not all trees. The overall stability of the algorithm is not affected.
2. Random forest algorithm performs equally well in case of numerical as well as categorical features.
3. You don't need to perform feature scaling in case of random forest algorithm since it doesn't rely on the distance between the data points in the feature space.

Cons of Random Forest Algorithm

1. One of the biggest disadvantages of random forest algorithm is its complexity. Since hundreds or sometimes thousands of trees are involved in prediction, it is not easy

to understand how the final prediction was made.

2. The complexity of an algorithm comes with the cost of time. Random forest algorithm can take a lot of time to execute depending upon the number of trees in the forest.

Implementing Random Forest Algorithm using Scikit Learn

In this section, we will use random forest algorithm to predict how much points can a player score in a basketball match based on his height, weight, percentage of successful field goals out of all attempts, percentage of successful throws out of all attempts. We have downloaded the dataset and it is available in the Datasets folder.

We will follow the same steps that we have been following in all the last chapters.

1- Importing Required Libraries

The following code imports required libraries:

```
import pandas as pd
import numpy as np
import matplotlib.pyplot as plt
%matplotlib inline
```

2- Importing the Dataset

Though the dataset is available online, we have downloaded it and added it in the dataset repository available with this book. The dataset name is "player.csv'. Execute the following command to import the dataset.

```
player_data =
pd.read_csv('D:\Datasets\playe
r.csv')
```

The script above reads the dataset and stores it in *player_data dataframe*.

3- Analyzing the Data

Execute the following script to eyeball the data:

```
player_data.head()
```

The output looks like this:

	Height	Weight	Field_Goals	Throws	Points
0	6.8	225	0.442	0.672	9.2
1	6.3	180	0.435	0.797	11.7
2	6.4	190	0.456	0.761	15.8
3	6.2	180	0.416	0.651	8.6
4	6.9	205	0.449	0.900	23.2

4- Data Preprocessing

To following script divides the data into feature and label set.

```
features = player_data.iloc[:,
0:4].values

labels = player_data.iloc[:,
4].values
```

Finally let's divide the data into 80 % training and 20% test sets:

```
from sklearn.model_selection
import train_test_split

train_features, test_features,
train_labels, test_labels =
```

```
train_test_split(features,
labels, test_size = 0.2,
random_state = 0)
```

5- Scaling the Data

If you look at the dataset it is not scaled well, for instance the Field_Goals and Throws column have values between 0 and 1, while the rest of the columns have higher values. Therefore, before training the algorithm, we will scale our data down. Remember we discussed scaling Chapter 3. Here we will use the standard scalar class.

```
from sklearn.preprocessing
import StandardScaler

feature_scaler =
StandardScaler()

train_features =
feature_scaler.fit_transform(t
rain_features)

test_features =
feature_scaler.transform(test_
features)
```

6- Training the Algorithm and making Predictions

To implement Random Forest Algorithm for regression tasks, the *RandomForestRegressor* class is of the *sklear.ensemble* library is used. The number of trees is passed as argument to the n_estimator parameter. In the following script the number of script is set to 200.

```
from sklearn.ensemble import
RandomForestRegressor


rf_reg =
RandomForestRegressor(n_estima
tors=200, random_state=0)
rf_reg.fit(train_features,
train_labels)
```

Execute the following script to predict the label for the test features:

```
predictions = rf_reg.predict(
test_features)
```

To compare predictions with real outputs, execute the following script:

Let's compare the predicted value with the actual values. Execute the following script to do so:

```
comparison=pd.DataFrame({'Real
':test_labels,
'Predictions':predictions})
print(comparison)
```

The output looks like this:

```
     Predictions   Real
0        10.6050   8.3
1         9.5780   7.2
2        10.0470   2.8
3        19.6975   5.6
4        16.0445   9.1
5        13.2735  15.8
6        12.8185   9.6
7        14.1255  15.4
8        11.8640   7.9
9        13.5840  11.7
10       13.9590  23.2
```

7- Evaluating the Algorithm

Execute the following script to find MAE, MSE and RMSE for our linear regression model.

```
from sklearn import metrics
print('MAE:',
metrics.mean_absolute_error(te
st_labels, predictions))
print('MSE:',
metrics.mean_squared_error(tes
t_labels, predictions))
print('RMSE:',
np.sqrt(metrics.mean_squared_e
rror(test_labels,
predictions)))
```

The output is always follows:

```
MAE: 5.00731818182
MSE: 39.4070574773
RMSE: 6.27750408023
```

The value of MAE is 5.00, which is greater than MAE value calculated for Linear Regression algorithm in Chapter 4 i.e. 4.65. Similarly, the value of RMSE in the case of

Random Forest algorithm is 6.27, which is greater than 5.67, i.e. the value obtained using Linear Regression algorithm in Chapter 4. Hence we can say that for predicting point scored by a basketball player given the dataset used in this chapter, Linear Regression algorithm outperforms the Random Forest algorithm.

Chapter 8

Support Vector Regression

Support Vector Regression (SVR) is a type of Support Vector Machines (SVM) Algorithm and can be used for performing linear as well as non-linear regression. Introduced in 1960's SVM is one of the most famous supervised machine learning algorithms. Before neural networks became common, SVM was said to be the most accurate machine learning algorithm.

In this chapter we will briefly review the intuition behind SVM algorithm and how they actually work. Since we are in regression section, we will implement SVR algorithm using Python library to predict the price of a car based on the year. But first let's study the theory behind SVM.

SVM Theory

For typical linear regression in two dimensional feature space, the task is to find a straight line that successfully bisects the data points. However in real world, there can be multiple decision boundaries that can successfully classify the data points as shown in Fig1.

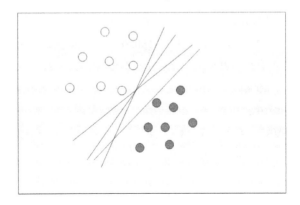

Fig1: Multiple boundaries

However whether a new data point will be successfully classified or not depends upon the decision boundary chosen for classification.

For instance take a look at Fig2. Suppose we have to classify new data point i.e. the Red Circle. If we have the decision boundary as in Fig2, the new data point will be classified as blue.

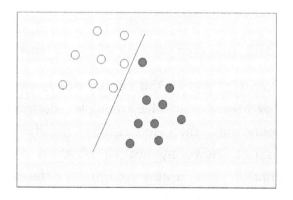

Fig2: New data point classified as blue

On the other hand if we have the decision boundary as in Fig3, the new data point will be classified as yellow as shown below:

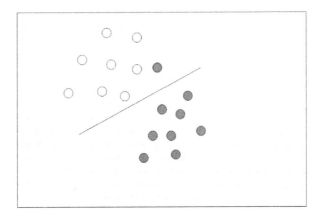

Fig3: New data point classified as yellow

From Fig2 and Fig3, it can be clearly seen that there can be multiple decision boundaries that successfully classify a dataset. However, not all of them are optimal. Given a new data point, different decision boundaries may classify data differently.

The job of SVM algorithm is to find the decision boundary that classifies data in such a way that the chances of misclassification can be minimized. SVM algorithm does so by maximizing the distance between the closest data points from all the classes in the dataset.

The SVM algorithm finds such a boundary with the help of support vectors, hence the name Support Vector Machines. Support vectors are the vectors that pass through the closest data points of the two classes to classify. The job is to maximize the distance between these two vectors. A line parallel to both these support vectors is drawn in the middle of these support vectors. This decision boundary is considered the most optimal decision boundary. The decision boundary found by Support Vector along with support vector machines looks like the one in Fig4.

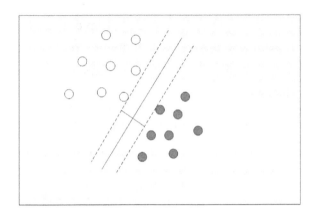

Fig4: Decision boundary with Support Vectors

Enough of the theory, now let's see how we can use Support Vector regression which is a type of SVM to predict price of a car based on year it was manufactured. We will use Python's Scikit Learn Library for that.

Implementing SVR with Python Scikit Learn

In this section we will use the "*car_price.csv*" dataset to predict the price of car (dependent variable) based on the year of manufacture (independent variable). You can find the dataset in the supplementary "Datasets" folder.

1- Importing Required Libraries

The following code imports required libraries:

```
import pandas as pd
import numpy as np
import matplotlib.pyplot as plt
%matplotlib inline
```

This script is implemented using Jupyter notebook. Therefore, to draw graphs within the notebook, we have used the command %matplotlib inline. If you are using Spyder, you can remove the last line.

2- Importing the Dataset

We will be using "car_price.csv" dataset. Execute the following script to import the dataset:

```
car_data =
pd.read_csv('D:\Datasets\car_p
rice.csv')
```

The script above reads the dataset and stores it in *car_data dataframe*.

3- Analyzing the Data

Let's first take a general look of our data. The *head* function returns the first 5 rows of the dataset. Execute the following script:

```
car_data.head()
```

	Year	Price
0	1980	2000
1	1985	3000
2	1983	2200
3	1990	3700
4	1995	4500

4- Data Preprocessing

To divide the data into features and labels, execute the following script:

```
features=
car_data.iloc[:,0:1].values
labels=
car_data.iloc[:,1].values
```

Finally let's divide the data into 80 % training and 20% test sets:

```
from sklearn.model_selection
import train_test_split
train_features, test_features,
train_labels, test_labels =
train_test_split(features,
labels, test_size = 0.2,
random_state = 0)
```

If you look at the dataset we can see that there is not a very huge difference between values of years and prices. Both of them have in thousands. Therefore, there is no need to scale the data and we can use this data as it is for training the algorithm.

5- Training the Algorithm and making Predictions

The *SVR* class of the *sklearn.svm* is used to implement support vector regression in

Python. The SVR class takes a value for its kernel parameter. If your data is linear which actually is the case with car_data, then use "linear" as kernel value, else you can use any kernel value from the list given in the documentations at this link.

SVR class has fit method that takes training features and labels as input and train the model as shown below:

```
from sklearn.svm import SVR
svr_reg = SVR(kernel='linear')
svr_reg.fit(train_features,
train_labels)
```

Finally, execute the following script to predict the label for the test features:

```
predictions = lin_reg.predict(
test_features)
```

All the predictions are stored in the *predictions* variable.

Let's compare the predicted value with the actual values. Execute the following script to do so:

```
comparison=pd.DataFrame({'Real
':test_labels,
'Predictions':predictions})

print(comparison)
```

```
     Predictions  Real
0         4945.0  5200
1         3699.0  3000
2         3610.0  3100
3         4055.0  4000
```

Evaluating the Algorithm

Execute the following script to find MAE, MSE and RMSE for our linear regression model.

```
from sklearn import metrics

print('MAE:',
metrics.mean_absolute_error(te
st_labels, predictions))
```

```
print('MSE:',
metrics.mean_squared_error(tes
t_labels, predictions))
print('RMSE:',
np.sqrt(metrics.mean_squared_e
rror(test_labels,
predictions)))
```

The output is always follows:

```
MAE: 379.75
MSE: 204187.75
RMSE: 451.871386569
```

The value of MAE is 379.75 in case of SVR, which is greater than MAE value calculated for Linear Regression algorithm in Chapter 4 i.e. 377.36 Similarly, the value of RMSE in the case of SVR calculate in this chapter is 451.87, which is greater than 397.89, i.e. the value obtained using Linear Regression algorithm in Chapter 4. Hence we can say that for car prices based on the year they were manufactured given the dataset used in this chapter, Linear Regression algorithm outperforms the Support Vector Regression Algorithm.

Chapter 9

Naïve Bayes Algorithm for Classification

In the previous chapters, we covered some of the most commonly used algorithms for regression e.g. Linear Regression, Support Vector Regression, Polynomial Regression, Decision Trees and Random Forest algorithms. Some of these algorithms have variants that can be used for classification as well which we will see in the upcoming chapters. In this chapter we will start our discussion about classification algorithms i.e. Algorithms used to predict discrete value, or a class label for input data. The first classification algorithm that we are going to cover in this section is the Naïve Bayes Algorithm.

Theory of Naïve Bayes (NB) Algorithm

Naïve Bayes algorithm is a supervised machine learning algorithm based on Bayes's Theorm. NB algorithm is based on principle of feature independence which states that features within a dataset have no relation to each other. For instance a fruit may be considered as banana if it is 5 or more inches long, yellow in color and 1 cm in diameter. Naïve Bayes have no concern if these features depend on each other. The fruit is declared as a banana via independent contribution of these features. Due to this independence assumption, NB algorithm is called Naïve.

Naïve Bayes algorithm is the simplest of all the machine learning algorithms and yet very powerful.

Mathematically Bayes theorem can be represented as:

$$P(A|B) = \frac{P(B|A).P(A)}{P(B)}$$

The aforementioned terms are explained as follows:

1- P(A|B) is the probability that event A will occur given attribute set B
2- P(A) is the prior probability of the occurrence of event A
3- P(B|A) is the probability of attribute set if the event A occurs
4- P(B) is the prior probability of the occurrence of predictors

Let's understand this concept with the help of an example.

Suppose we have weight profile of 12 individuals and based on that we want to predict whether or not the patients are diabetic. The record set looks like this:

Weight	Diabetic
Overweight	Yes
Normal	No
Underweight	No
Normal	Yes
Overweight	Yes
Normal	No
Underweight	No
Overweight	No
Normal	No
Overweight	Yes
Underweight	No

Underweight	No

There are three steps involved in manually implementing the NB algorithm.

1- Create a frequency table for the data as shown below:

	Yes	No
Overweight	3	1
Normal	1	3
Underweight	0	4
Total	4	8

2- Calculate the Class/Event Prior Probability and Attribute Prior Probability

No let's calculate the prior probability of the events:

P(A) when Diabetic (Yes) = 4/12 = 0.33

P(A) when Diabetic (No) = 8/12 = 0.67

Finally let's find the prior probability of the features:

P(B) when Overweight = 4/12 = 0.33

P(B) when Normal= 4/12 = 0.33

P(B) when Underweight = 4/12 = 0.33

3- Now if a new patient comes, we have to find whether he is diabetic depending upon his weight. There can be two outcomes: diabetic or not. We will find probabilities for both. The class that results in higher probability will be assigned to the patient.

Suppose an overweight patient arrives to the clinic and we have to test him for diabetes. We need to solve two equations:

a) P(Yes|Overweight)   =
   P(Overweight|Yes)   x   P(Yes)   /
   P(Overweight)

   = (0.75 X 0.33) / 0.33

   = 0.75

b) P(No|Overweight) = P(Overweight|No) x P(No) / P(Overweight)

   = (0.125 X 0.67) / 0.33

   = 0.25

You can see that probability of being diabetic when overweight is 0.75 which is greater than probability of not being diabetic which is 0.25, therefore NB algorithm will classify this patient as diabetic.

In the above case there was only one attribute, in case of multiple attributes, the probability can be calculated as:

$P(A|B) = P(B1|A) \times P(B2|A) \times P(B3|A)$ ....
$P(BN|A) \times P(A)$

Advantages of Naïve Bayes Algorithm

1. NB algorithm is very simple and fast to train since no complex mathematics and error correction or back propagations is involved.

2. NB algorithms outperform most of the other algorithms in case of categorical data. For numeric features, NB algorithm assumes normal distribution.

Disadvantages of Naïve Bayes Algorithm

1. In real world data, features are mostly dependent on other features. The independence assumption of NB algorithm makes it a bad predictor for datasets with interdependent features.

2. If a categorical feature has such a value in test set which was not seen

in the training set, the NB algorithm will assign zero probability to such instance. Therefore, it is very important to cross validate results obtained using NB algorithm.

3.

Naïve Bayes Algorithm Applications

1. NB algorithm is ideal for multi-class problems and is commonly employed for text classification problems such as sentimental analysis and email spam filtering.
2. NB algorithm is also widely used in combination of collaborative filtering algorithms for building machine learning based recommender systems.
3. NB is extremely fast compared to other advanced algorithms and is therefore incorporated in real time applications.

Implementing Naïve Bayes Algorithm With Python Scikit Learn

As always, in this section we will use Python's Scikit Learn library to implement the Naïve Bayes algorithm.

In Scikit Learn you can implement three variants of NB algorithm:

1. Guassian NB: Use feature has normal data distribution
2. Multinomial NB: Use when your features contain discrete data
3. Bernoulli: Use when your features contain binary data.

In this section, we will predict the type of the iris flower based on four attributes: sepal length, sepal width, petal length and petal width.

More details of the IRIS dataset can be found at this link:

https://archive.ics.uci.edu/ml/datasets/Iris

The dataset has been supplied with the book and can be found by the name of iris_data.csv in the Datasets folder.

Now you should be familiar with rest of the steps. We start by importing the libraries:

7- Importing Required Libraries

The following code imports required libraries:

```
import pandas as pd
import numpy as np
import matplotlib.pyplot as plt
%matplotlib inline
```

8- Importing the Dataset

Execute the following command to import the dataset.

```
iris_data =
pd.read_csv('D:\Datasets\iris_
data.csv')
```

The script above reads the dataset and stores it in *iris_data dataframe*.

9- Analyzing the Data

Execute the following script to eyeball the data:

```
iris_data.head()
```

The output looks like this:

	sepal_length	sepal_width	petal_length	petal_width	species
0	5.1	3.5	1.4	0.2	setosa
1	4.9	3.0	1.4	0.2	setosa
2	4.7	3.2	1.3	0.2	setosa
3	4.6	3.1	1.5	0.2	setosa
4	5.0	3.6	1.4	0.2	setosa

10- Data Preprocessing

To following script divides the data into feature and label set.

```
features = player_data.iloc[:,
0:4].values
labels = player_data.iloc[:,
4].values
```

Finally let's divide the data into 80 % training and 20% test sets:

```
from sklearn.model_selection
import train_test_split
```

```
train_features, test_features,
train_labels, test_labels =
train_test_split(features,
labels, test_size = 0.2,
random_state = 0)
```

11- Scaling the Data

If you look at the dataset it is not scaled well, for instance the petal_width column have values between 0 and 1, while the rest of the columns have higher values. Therefore, before training the algorithm, we will scale our data down. Remember we discussed scaling in the 3rd chapter. Here we will use the standard scalar class.

```
from sklearn.preprocessing
import StandardScaler

feature_scaler =
StandardScaler()

train_features =
feature_scaler.fit_transform(t
rain_features)

test_features =
feature_scaler.transform(test_
features)
```

12- Training the Algorithm and making Predictions

We can see that we have normal distribution for the feature values; therefore we can use Gaussian Naïve Bayes for this problem. To implement Gaussian Naïve Algorithm with Scikit learn we need to use the *GaussianNB* class of the *sklear.naive_bayes* library. Execute the following script to train the model on train_features and train_labels

```
 from sklearn.naive_bayes
import GaussianNB
nb_clf = GaussianNB()
nb_clf.fit(train_features,
train_labels)
```

Execute the following script to predict the label for the test features:

```
predictions = nb_clf.predict(
test_features)
```

To compare predictions with real outputs, execute the following script:

```
comparison=pd.DataFrame({'Real
':test_labels,
'Predictions':predictions})
```

```
print(comparison)
```

The output looks like this:

```
      Predictions          Real
 0      virginica     virginica
 1     versicolor    versicolor
 2        setosa        setosa
 3      virginica     virginica
 4        setosa        setosa
 5      virginica     virginica
 6        setosa        setosa
 7     versicolor    versicolor
 8     versicolor    versicolor
 9     versicolor    versicolor
10     versicolor     virginica
11     versicolor    versicolor
12     versicolor    versicolor
13     versicolor    versicolor
14     versicolor    versicolor
15        setosa        setosa
16     versicolor    versicolor
17     versicolor    versicolor
18        setosa        setosa
19        setosa        setosa
20      virginica     virginica
21     versicolor    versicolor
22        setosa        setosa
23        setosa        setosa
24      virginica     virginica
25        setosa        setosa
26        setosa        setosa
27     versicolor    versicolor
28     versicolor    versicolor
29        setosa        setosa
```

It can be seen from the output that our
algorithm did a tremendous job of predicting
the flower type. Out of the 30 test instances,
29 have been predicted correctly, while only

one (highlighted in red) has been misclassified.

Evaluating the Algorithm

To evaluate regression algorithms we used mean absolute error, root mean squared error, and mean squared error. For classification problems the performance metrics are different. Normally Precision, Recall and F1 measures are used to evaluate the performance of classification algorithms. Let's briefly review Confusion Matrix, Accuracy Precision, Recall and F1 Measures are:

Confusion Matrix:

A confusion matrix is a matrix that displays true positive, true negative, false positive and false positive predicted values.

True positives (TP) are those values which are actually positive and they are also predicted positive. Similarly, True Negatives (TN) are those values which are actually negative and predicted negative.

On the other hand, False Positives are the values which are actually negative but have been falsely predicted as positive. Similarly, False Negatives are those which are actually positive but falsely predicted as negative.

A confusion matrix looks like this:

	Actual Positive	Actual Negative
Predicted Positive	True Positive	False Positive
Predicted Negative	False Negative	True Negative

Accuracy:

The simplest parameter to evaluate the performance of a machine learning algorithm is Accuracy. Accuracy refers to the number of correctly predicted instance divided the total number of instances. Mathematically it can be represented as:

$$\text{Accuracy} = (TP + TN) / (TP + FP + TN + FN)$$

Precision:

Precision refers to the ability of an algorithm to make precise predictions. It can be calculated by dividing the true positives by predicted positives (true positives + false positives) Mathematically it is represented as:

$$\text{Precision} = TP / (TP + FP)$$

Recall

Recall can be calculated by dividing the true positives by actual number of positives (true positive + false negative)

$$\text{Recall} = TP / (TP + FN)$$

F1 – Measure

F1 measure is the harmonic mean of precision and recall

Like regression performance metrics, we do not have to calculate the values for the aforementioned metrics by hand. Python Scikit Learn library comes with classes that can be used for this purpose. Execute the following script to see the performance of NB algorithm that we trained to predict iris flower type:

```
from sklearn.metrics import
classification_report,
confusion_matrix,
accuracy_score

print(confusion_matrix(test_la
bels, predictions))

print(classification_report(te
st_labels, predictions))

print(accuracy_score(test_labe
ls, predictions))
```

The output for the script above looks like this:

```
[[11  0  0]
 [ 0 13  0]
 [ 0  1  5]]
              precision    recall  f1-score   support

      setosa       1.00      1.00      1.00        11
  versicolor       0.93      1.00      0.96        13
   virginica       1.00      0.83      0.91         6

 avg / total       0.97      0.97      0.97        30

0.966666666667
```

From the output it can be seen that our algorithm achieved an accuracy of 96.66%.

Conclusion

In this chapter, we started our discussion about the classification algorithms. The first classification algorithm that we studied in this Chapter is the Naïve Bayes Algorithm. We saw the theory behind the algorithm and its implementation with Python.

Chapter 10

K Nearest Neighbors Algorithm for Classification

In the last Chapter, we studied Naïve Bayes algorithm for classification. We said that NB algorithm assumes feature independence. Furthermore, one of the drawbacks of the NB algorithm is that it assumes that categorical feature values are normally distributed. However in most of the cases, real world data doesn't follow any trend e.g. uniform distribution or linear separatability etc. In such cases a non-parametric algorithm can come handy. K Nearest Neighbors (KNN) algorithm is one such non-parametric algorithm.

Theory of KNN

The intuition behind KNN algorithm is extremely simple. KNN algorithm simply finds the distance between the new test data points from all the other data points in the dataset. It then ranks all the other data points in ascending order of their according to their distance with the test point. Finally it chooses the top K nearest data points. It then assigns the new data point to the class of the majority of K data points. Now you should know that why scale our data down so that the distance between the different dimensions of the data points remain distance. Distance can be Manhattan as well as Euclidean depending upon the problem.

Let's visually see the working of a KNN algorithm.

Suppose we have some data points in two dimensional space, divided into two categories: red and blue as shown in the following figure.

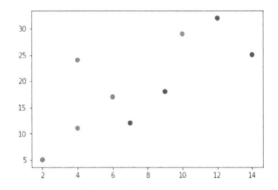

Now if we have to classify a new data point. We will calculate its distance from all the red and blue data points. Then we will choose K nearest data points. Suppose new data point is yellow circle and the value of K is three as shown below:

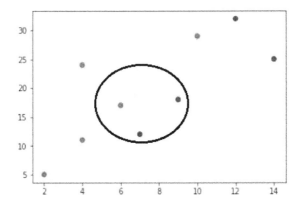

You can see that out of the three nearest neighbors of the yellow data point, two are blue and one is red. Therefore, the yellow data point will be classified in the blue class.

KNN algorithm has no training phase; in fact it uses whole dataset for classifying a new data point. It is for this purpose, it is known as lazy learning algorithm.

Advantages of KNN Algorithm

1. Unlike other algorithms, the list of parameters required by KNN algorithm is not very exhaustive. You only need to specify the number of nearest neighbor K and the type of distance function.

2. KNN algorithm is extremely fast when compared to logistic regression, decision trees and other classification algorithm since there is no training phase involved in KNN. New data point can directly be classified without extensive training, simply by finding its distance from the other data points.

3. KNN is very simple and easy to implement. Furthermore, new data points can be added at any time anytime since whenever a prediction has to be made, distance with all the data points is recalculated.

Disadvantages of KNN Algorithm

1. KNN algorithm work well with numerical features but in case of categorical features, its performance decreases. This is because for categorical features, the distance between two data points cannot be calculated precisely.

2. Prediction cost of KNN algorithm increases with increase in the size of the data and dimensions because it is time consuming to calculate distance between large number of data points with high dimensions.

KNN Implementation with Scikit Learn

In this section we will implement the KNN algorithm with Python's Scikit Learn library. The problem that we are going to solve with KNN algorithm is predicting whether a bank currency note is genuine or not. We have four attributes in the dataset i.e. entropy, skewness, variance and curtosis of the wavelet transformed image of the currency note.

More details about the dataset can be found at this link.

The dataset has been supplied with the book and can be found by the name of banknote_data.csv in the Datasets folder.

As always we start by importing the libraries:

13- Importing Required Libraries

The following code imports required libraries:

```
import pandas as pd
import numpy as np
import matplotlib.pyplot as plt
%matplotlib inline
```

14- Importing the Dataset

Execute the following command to import the dataset.

```
banknote_data =
pd.read_csv(r'D:\Datasets\bank note_data.csv')
```

The script above reads the dataset and stores it in *banknote_data dataframe*.

15- Analyzing the Data

The following script returns the data dimensions:

```
banknote_data.shape
```

The above script returns (1372, 5) which means that our dataset contains 1372 records and five attributes.

Execute the following script to eyeball the data:

```
banknote_data.head()
```

The output looks like this:

	Variance	Skewness	Curtosis	Entropy	Class
0	3.62160	8.6661	-2.8073	-0.44699	0
1	4.54590	8.1674	-2.4586	-1.46210	0
2	3.86600	-2.6383	1.9242	0.10645	0
3	3.45660	9.5228	-4.0112	-3.59440	0
4	0.32924	-4.4552	4.5718	-0.98880	0

16- Data Preprocessing

To following script divides the data into feature and label set.

```
features=
banknote_data.iloc[:,0:4].valu
es
```

```
labels=
banknote_data.iloc[:,4].values
```

Finally let's divide the data into 80 % training and 20% test sets:

```
from sklearn.model_selection
import train_test_split

train_features, test_features,
train_labels, test_labels =
train_test_split(features,
labels, test_size = 0.2,
random_state = 0)
```

17- Scaling the Data

If you are using KNN algorithm , it is always a good practice to scale your data. Remember we discussed scaling in the 3rd chapter. Here we will use the standard scalar class.

```
from sklearn.preprocessing
import StandardScaler

feature_scaler =
StandardScaler()

train_features =
feature_scaler.fit_transform(t
rain_features)
```

```
test_features =
feature_scaler.transform(test_
features)
```

18- Training the Algorithm and making Predictions

To implement KNN Algorithm with Scikit learn we need to use the *KNeighborsClassifier* class of the *sklear.neighbors* library. The value of K is specified as value for the *n_neighbors* parameter as shown in the following script. We use a value of 3 for K. Execute the following script to train the model on train_features and train_labels

```
 from sklearn.neighbors import
KNeighborsClassifier
knn_clf =
KNeighborsClassifier(n_neighbo
rs=3)
knn_clf.fit(train_features,
train_labels)
```

Execute the following script to predict the label for the test features:

```
predictions = nb_clf.predict(
test_features)
```

To compare predictions with real outputs, execute the following script:

```
comparison=pd.DataFrame({'Real
':test_labels,
'Predictions':predictions})
```

```
print(comparison)
```

The output looks like this:

	Predictions	Real
0	1	1
1	0	0
2	1	1
3	0	0
4	0	0
5	0	0
6	0	0
7	0	0
8	1	1
9	1	1
10	0	0
11	0	0
12	1	1
13	0	0
14	0	0
15	0	0
16	1	1
17	1	1
18	0	0
19	0	0
20	1	1
21	0	0
22	0	0
23	1	1
24	0	0
25	1	1
26	0	0
27	1	1

You can see that most of our predictions are accurate.

Evaluating the Algorithm

From the last chapter, we know that to evaluate performance of classification algorithms we can use confusion matrix, accuracy, precision, and recall and F1 measure as metrics. Execute the following script to find the values for these metrics:

```
from sklearn.metrics import
classification_report,
confusion_matrix,
accuracy_score

print(confusion_matrix(test_la
bels, predictions))

print(classification_report(te
st_labels, predictions))

print(accuracy_score(test_labe
ls, predictions))
```

The output of the script above looks like this:

```
[[157   0]
 [  0 118]]
            precision    recall  f1-score   support

         0       1.00      1.00      1.00       157
         1       1.00      1.00      1.00       118

avg / total       1.00      1.00      1.00       275

1.0
```

It can be seen from the output that our algorithm did a pretty good job at predicting the authenticity of bank note. We got 100% accuracy.

Effect of Value of K on Prediction Accuracy

In the previous section, we randomly set the value of K to 3 which incidentally resulted in 100% accuracy. However, this is not always the case. We don't know the best value of K from the outset. The best way to find the value of K is to try different values of K and choose the value that result in highest accuracy.

In the script below will again predict the authentication of currency note by using values of k between 1 and 50. Execute the following script:

```
rate_of_error = []


for i in range(1, 50):
    knn =
KNeighborsClassifier(n_neighbors=i)
    knn.fit(train_features,
train_labels)
```

```
    predictions =
knn.predict(test_features)
```

```
rate_of_error.append(np.mean(p
redictions != test_labels))
```

Once errors are calculated per value of K, a
chart can be printed showing the error rates
with change in value of K. Execute the
following script:

```
  plt.figure(figsize=(10, 5))
```

```
plt.plot(range(1, 50),
rate_of_error, color='green',
linestyle='solid', marker='o',
```

```
markerfacecolor='red',
markersize=10)
```

```
plt.title('K value vs Error')
```

```
plt.xlabel('K Value')
```

```
plt.ylabel('Error Value')
```

The output looks like this:

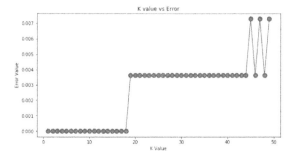

From the above picture, it is clear that the error remains at zero for all the values of K between 1 and 18. After 18, the error increases to 4% which still not huge.

Conclusion

In this chapter, we covered K Nearest Neighbor algorithm for classification. We studied the theory behind K Nearest Neighbors algorithm and then implemented the algorithm to solve the problem of bank note authentication. In the next chapter we will see how we can use Decision Tree algorithm for classification Tasks.

Chapter 11

Decision Tree for Classification

In chapter 6, "Decision Tree for Regression" we studied how a decision tree works and what are the steps involved in the decision making process of a decision tree. However, in Chapter 6 we used decision tree for regression tasks i.e. for predicting petrol prices. In addition to regression, we can also use decision tree for classification tasks. This is what we are going to do in this chapter. This chapter will be fairly brief since we have covered decision tree in detail in Chapter 6. Here we will just see an example of how decision tree solves classification problem with the help of Python's Scikit Learn Library.

Solving Classification Problems with Decision Tree in Python Scikit Learn

In Chapter 9, we predicted the type of Iris flower using Naïve Bayes Algorithm. Let's try to solve the same classification task with the help of decision tree algorithm.

We start by importing the libraries:

1- Importing Required Libraries

The following code imports required libraries:

```
import pandas as pd
import numpy as np
import matplotlib.pyplot as plt
%matplotlib inline
```

2- Importing the Dataset

Execute the following command to import the dataset.

```
iris_data =
pd.read_csv('D:\Datasets\iris_
data.csv')
```

The script above reads the dataset and stores it in *iris_data dataframe*.

3- Analyzing the Data

Execute the following script to eyeball the data:

```
iris_data.head()
```

The output looks like this:

	sepal_length	sepal_width	petal_length	petal_width	species
0	5.1	3.5	1.4	0.2	setosa
1	4.9	3.0	1.4	0.2	setosa
2	4.7	3.2	1.3	0.2	setosa
3	4.6	3.1	1.5	0.2	setosa
4	5.0	3.6	1.4	0.2	setosa

4- Data Preprocessing

To following script divides the data into feature and label set.

```
features = iris_data.iloc[:, 0:4].values
labels = iris_data.iloc[:, 4].values
```

Finally let's divide the data into 80 % training and 20% test sets:

```
from sklearn.model_selection import train_test_split
```

```
train_features, test_features,
train_labels, test_labels =
train_test_split(features,
labels, test_size = 0.2,
random_state = 0)
```

5- Scaling the Data

If you look at the dataset it is not scaled well, for instance the petal_width column have values between 0 and 1, while the rest of the columns have higher values. Therefore, before training the algorithm, we will scale our data down. Remember we discussed scaling in the 3rd chapter. Here we will use the standard scalar class.

```
from sklearn.preprocessing
import StandardScaler

feature_scaler =
StandardScaler()

train_features =
feature_scaler.fit_transform(t
rain_features)

test_features =
feature_scaler.transform(test_
features)
```

6- Training the Algorithm and making Predictions

We can see that we have normal distribution for the feature values; therefore we can use Gaussian Naïve Bayes for this problem. To implement Gaussian Naïve Algorithm with Scikit learn we need to use the *DecisionTreeClassifier* class of the *sklear.tree* library. Execute the following script to train the model on train_features and train_labels

```
from sklearn.tree import
DecisionTreeClassifier
dt_clf =
DecisionTreeClassifier(random_
state=0)
dt_clf.fit(train_features,
train_labels)
```

Execute the following script to predict the label for the test features:

```
predictions = dt_clf.predict(
test_features)
```

To compare predictions with real outputs, execute the following script:

```
comparison=pd.DataFrame({'Real
':test_labels,
'Predictions':predictions})
print(comparison)
```

The output looks like this:

```
     Predictions       Real
0      virginica   virginica
1     versicolor  versicolor
2         setosa      setosa
3      virginica   virginica
4         setosa      setosa
5      virginica   virginica
6         setosa      setosa
7     versicolor  versicolor
8     versicolor  versicolor
9     versicolor  versicolor
10     virginica   virginica
11    versicolor  versicolor
12    versicolor  versicolor
13    versicolor  versicolor
14    versicolor  versicolor
15        setosa      setosa
16    versicolor  versicolor
17    versicolor  versicolor
18        setosa      setosa
19        setosa      setosa
20     virginica   virginica
21    versicolor  versicolor
22        setosa      setosa
23        setosa      setosa
24     virginica   virginica
25        setosa      setosa
26        setosa      setosa
27    versicolor  versicolor
28    versicolor  versicolor
```

Evaluating the Algorithm

The following script returns values for performance metrics of our classification algorithm:

```
from sklearn.metrics import
classification_report,
```

```
confusion_matrix,
accuracy_score

print(confusion_matrix(test_la
bels, predictions))

print(classification_report(te
st_labels, predictions))

print(accuracy_score(test_labe
ls, predictions))
```

The output looks like this:

```
[[11  0  0]
 [ 0 13  0]
 [ 0  0  6]]
              precision    recall  f1-score   support

      setosa       1.00      1.00      1.00        11
  versicolor       1.00      1.00      1.00        13
   virginica       1.00      1.00      1.00         6

 avg / total       1.00      1.00      1.00        30

1.0
```

From the output it can be seen that 100% prediction accuracy has been achieved using decision tree algorithm which is greater than 96.66% achieved using Naïve Bayes algorithm in Chapter 9

Conclusion

In this chapter we studied how decision tree algorithm can be used for classification tasks. In the next chapter we will study how random forest algorithm can also be used to perform classification tasks.

Chapter 12

Random Forest for Classification

In chapter 7, we studied the details of Random Forest Algorithm and saw its pros and cons. We also implemented Random Forest algorithm in Python Scikit Learn to solve regression problem. However, we can also use Random Forest algorithm for classification problems. Since we are in classification section, it makes sense to add a chapter dedicated to Random Forest algorithm for classification.

We will not go into the theory of Random Forest algorithm here since it has already been covered in Chapter 7. We will straight jump into the code section. As always we will use Python's Scikit Learn Library to implement Random Forest Algorithm for classification.

Implementing Random Forest Classification with Python's Scikit Learn

The problem that we are going to solve with Random Forest algorithm is predicting whether a bank currency note is genuine or not. This is the same problem that we solved in Chapter 10 (KNN Algorithm). We have four attributes in the dataset i.e. entropy, skewness, variance and curtosis of the wavelet transformed image of the currency note.

More details about the dataset can be found at this link.

The dataset has been supplied with the book and can be found by the name of banknote_data.csv in the Datasets folder. Follow these steps

1- Importing Required Libraries

```
import pandas as pd

import numpy as np

import matplotlib.pyplot as
plt

%matplotlib inline
```

2- Importing the Dataset

The following script imports the dataset.

```
banknote_data =
pd.read_csv(r'D:\Datasets\bank
note_data.csv')
```

The script above reads the dataset and stores it in *banknote_data dataframe*.

3- Analyzing the Data

The following script returns the data dimensions:

```
banknote_data.shape
```

The above script returns (1372, 5) which means that our dataset contains 1372 records and five attributes.

To see how the data looks like, execute the following script. It returns the first five rows of the data.

```
banknote_data.head()
```

The output looks like this:

	Variance	Skewness	Curtosis	Entropy	Class
0	3.62160	8.6661	-2.8073	-0.44699	0
1	4.54590	8.1674	-2.4586	-1.46210	0
2	3.86600	-2.6383	1.9242	0.10645	0
3	3.45660	9.5228	-4.0112	-3.59440	0
4	0.32924	-4.4552	4.5718	-0.98880	0

4- Data Preprocessing

To following script divides the data into feature and label set.

```
features=
banknote_data.iloc[:,0:4].valu
es
labels=
banknote_data.iloc[:,4].values
```

Finally let's divide the data into 80 % training and 20% test sets:

```
from sklearn.model_selection
import train_test_split

train_features, test_features,
train_labels, test_labels =
train_test_split(features,
labels, test_size = 0.2,
random_state = 0)
```

5- Scaling the Data

For Random Forest algorithm, it is not necessary to scale the data, however just for the sake of practice, let's scale the data using standard scalar. Remember we discussed scaling in the 3rd chapter.

```
from sklearn.preprocessing
import StandardScaler

feature_scaler =
StandardScaler()

train_features =
feature_scaler.fit_transform(t
rain_features)

test_features =
feature_scaler.transform(test_
features)
```

6- Training the Algorithm and making Predictions

To solve regression problems with Random Forest, we can use *RandomForestRegressor* class of the *sklearn.ensemble* library. For classification problems we need to use *RandomForestClassifier* class of the same library. Execute the following script to train the model on train_features and train_labels.

```
 from sklearn.ensemble import
RandomForestClassifier


rf_clf =
RandomForestClassifier(n_estim
ators=50, random_state=0)
rf_clf.fit(train_features,
train_labels)
```

Execute the following script to predict the label for the test features:

```
predictions = rf_clf .predict(
test_features)
```

To compare predictions with real outputs, execute the following script:

```
comparison=pd.DataFrame({'Real
':test_labels,
'Predictions':predictions})

print(comparison)
```

A snippet of the output looks like this:

```
     Predictions   Real
0             1       1
1             0       0
2             1       1
3             0       0
4             0       0
5             0       0
6             0       0
7             0       0
8             1       1
9             1       1
10            0       0
11            0       0
12            1       1
13            0       0
14            0       0
15            0       0
16            1       1
17            1       1
18            0       0
19            0       0
20            1       1
21            0       0
22            0       0
23            1       1
24            0       0
25            1       1
26            0       0
```

7- Evaluating the Algorithm

405

We know that to evaluate performance of classification algorithms we can use confusion matrix, accuracy, precision, and recall and F1 measure as metrics. Execute the following script to find the values for these metrics:

```
from sklearn.metrics import
classification_report,
confusion_matrix,
accuracy_score

print(confusion_matrix(test_la
bels, predictions))

print(classification_report(te
st_labels, predictions))

print(accuracy_score(test_labe
ls, predictions))
```

The output of the script above looks like this:

```
[[155   2]
 [  1 117]]
             precision    recall  f1-score   support

          0       0.99      0.99      0.99       157
          1       0.98      0.99      0.99       118

avg / total       0.99      0.99      0.99       275

0.989090909091
```

From the above output it can be seen that we have three wrong predictions in case of Random Forest classification. For KNN we had zero wrong predictions. Try to change the value for the number of estimators and see if you can get better results with Random Forest algorithm or not.

Conclusion

In this Chapter we saw how Random Forest algorithm can be used to solve classification problem. In the next chapter, we will see how Support Vector Machines algorithm can be used to solve classification problems.

Chapter 13

Support Vector Machines for Classification

In Chapter 8, we studied Support Vector Regression algorithm which is a variant of Support Vector Machines (SVM) algorithm and is used to solve regression problems. We studied the theory of SVM algorithm and also saw what are the pros and cons of SVM algorithm in Chapter 8 in detail. In this Chapter we will see how SVM algorithm can be used to solve classification problems. We will not focus on theoretical details of SVM in this Chapter since they have already been covered in Chapter 8. Here we will see how we can implement SVM algorithm in Python to solve classification problem.

SVM for classification using Python's Scikit Learn

In Chapter 9 and 11, we predicted the type of Iris flower using Naïve Bayes Algorithm and Decision Trees algorithm, respectively. Let's try to solve the same classification task with the help of Support Vector Machines algorithm.

We start by importing the libraries:

1- Importing Required Libraries

The following code imports required libraries:

```
import pandas as pd
import numpy as np
import matplotlib.pyplot as plt
%matplotlib inline
```

2- Importing the Dataset

Execute the following command to import the dataset.

```
iris_data =
pd.read_csv('D:\Datasets\iris_
data.csv')
```

The script above reads the dataset and stores it in *iris_data dataframe*.

3- Analyzing the Data

Execute the following script to eyeball the data:

```
iris_data.head()
```

The output looks like this:

	sepal_length	sepal_width	petal_length	petal_width	species
0	5.1	3.5	1.4	0.2	setosa
1	4.9	3.0	1.4	0.2	setosa
2	4.7	3.2	1.3	0.2	setosa
3	4.6	3.1	1.5	0.2	setosa
4	5.0	3.6	1.4	0.2	setosa

4- Data Preprocessing

To following script divides the data into feature and label set.

```
features = iris_data.iloc[:,
0:4].values
```

```
labels = iris_data.iloc[:,
4].values
```

Finally let's divide the data into 80 %
training and 20% test sets:

```
from sklearn.model_selection
import train_test_split

train_features, test_features,
train_labels, test_labels =
train_test_split(features,
labels, test_size = 0.2,
random_state = 0)
```

5- Scaling the Data

If you look at the dataset it is not scaled well,
for instance the petal_width column have
values between 0 and 1, while the rest of the
columns have higher values. Therefore,
before training the algorithm, we will scale
our data down.

```
from sklearn.preprocessing
import StandardScaler

feature_scaler =
StandardScaler()

train_features =
feature_scaler.fit_transform(t
rain_features)
```

```
test_features =
feature_scaler.transform(test_
features)
```

6- Training the Algorithm and making Predictions

In case of regression we used *SVR* class of the *sklearn.svm* library. For classification we need to use *SVC* class of the same library. Execute the following script to train the model on train_features and train_labels

```
from sklearn.svm import SVC
svm_clf = SVC()
svm_clf.fit(train_features,
train_labels)
```

Execute the following script to predict the label for the test features:

```
predictions =
svm_clf.fit.predict(
test_features)
```

To compare predictions with real outputs, execute the following script:

```
comparison=pd.DataFrame({'Real
':test_labels,
'Predictions':predictions})
```

```
print(comparison)
```

The output looks like this:

```
      Predictions         Real
0       virginica     virginica
1      versicolor    versicolor
2          setosa        setosa
3       virginica     virginica
4          setosa        setosa
5       virginica     virginica
6          setosa        setosa
7      versicolor    versicolor
8      versicolor    versicolor
9      versicolor    versicolor
10      virginica     virginica
11     versicolor    versicolor
12     versicolor    versicolor
13     versicolor    versicolor
14     versicolor    versicolor
15         setosa        setosa
16     versicolor    versicolor
17     versicolor    versicolor
18         setosa        setosa
19         setosa        setosa
20      virginica     virginica
21     versicolor    versicolor
22         setosa        setosa
23         setosa        setosa
24      virginica     virginica
25         setosa        setosa
26         setosa        setosa
27     versicolor    versicolor
28     versicolor    versicolor
```

Evaluating the Algorithm

The following script returns values for performance metrics of our classification algorithm:

```
from sklearn.metrics import
classification_report,
```

```
confusion_matrix,
accuracy_score

print(confusion_matrix(test_la
bels, predictions))

print(classification_report(te
st_labels, predictions))

print(accuracy_score(test_labe
ls, predictions))
```

The output looks like this:

```
[[11  0  0]
 [ 0 13  0]
 [ 0  0  6]]
              precision    recall  f1-score   support

      setosa       1.00      1.00      1.00        11
  versicolor       1.00      1.00      1.00        13
   virginica       1.00      1.00      1.00         6

 avg / total       1.00      1.00      1.00        30

1.0
```

From the output it can be seen that 100% prediction accuracy has been achieved using decision tree algorithm which is greater than 96.66% achieved using Naïve Bayes algorithm in Chapter 9 and is equal to the accuracy achieved using Decision Tree classification algorithm in Chapter 11.

Conclusion

With this section we are going to end the Classification section of our supervised machine learning Part of the book. In the next chapter we will start studying unsupervised machine learning. In unsupervised machine learning we will study two clustering algorithms i.e. K-Means Clustering and Hierarchical Clustering. Happy Coding!!!

Chapter 14

K Means Clustering Algorithm

In the previous chapters we covered Supervised Machine Learning. We saw Regression and Classification that are the two main types of Supervised Learning. In this chapter and the next, we will cover Unsupervised Machine Learning i.e. learning from unlabeled data. In this Chapter we will study K-Means clustering algorithm.

K Means algorithm is one of the most widely used unsupervised machine learning algorithm used for clustering data points based on their similarity measure.

Steps of K-Mean Clustering

K-Means clustering algorithm is extremely simple and easy to understand. Following are the steps involved in K-Means clustering:

1- Randomly choose the number of centroids K. Where K corresponds to the number of clusters that you want your data grouped to.

2- Find the distance between all the data points and all the centroids. The distance can be Euclidean or Manhattan but normally Euclidean distance is used.

3- Assign the data points to the centroid with least distance. Repeat this step for all the data points forming K clusters of points.

4- Update the location of each centroid by taking mean of x and y components of all the points in the cluster.

5- Repeat steps 2, 3 and 4 until updated positions of all the centroids are same as their previous positions.

Luckily for us, we don't have to perform all these steps manually. We can simply use Python's Scikit Learn library for clustering tasks as well.

K-Means Clustering With Python's Scikit Learn

In Chapter 4, Regression, we predicted the price of cars based on their year of manufacturing. In this section we will see how we cluster those cars into different clusters based on similarities. So let's start clustering.

1. Importing Libraries

As always, the first step is to import required libraries:

```
import pandas as pd
import numpy as np
import matplotlib.pyplot as plt
%matplotlib inline
```

2. Importing Data

The following script imports the data:

```
car_data                         =
pd.read_csv('D:\Datasets\car_p
rice.csv')
```

3. Data Analysis

Execute the following script to see how our dataset looks like:

```
car_data.head()
```

The output looks like this:

	Year	Price
0	1980	2000
1	1985	3000
2	1983	2200
3	1990	3700
4	1995	4500

Finally, lets plot the data and see if can find any clusters in the dataset. Execute the following script:

```
plt.scatter(car_data['Year'],
car_data['Price'])
plt.title("Year vs Price")
plt.xlabel("Year")
plt.ylabel("Price")
plt.show()
```

The output of the script above looks like this:

If we look at the above graph we do not find any visible clusters. However if we are tasked with dividing the above data points into three clusters, we might form a cluster of cars with low price and very old models (points at the bottom left), a cluster of cars with medium price and old models (points in the middle of the chart) and a cluster of cars that are relatively new and have higher prices (points at the top right). Let's try to divide the above data points into three clusters using Python's Sklearn Library.

4. Clustering the Data

To implement K-Means clustering with sklearn, the *KMeans* class of the *sklearn.cluster* library is used. The number of clusters can be defined by *n_cluster* parameter of *KMeans* class. In the script below, we create three clusters. The *fit* method is then called to cluster the data as shown in the following script:

```
from sklearn.cluster import KMeans
km_clus = KMeans(n_clusters=3)
km_clus.fit(car_data)
```

Now to find the centroids found by our clustering algorithm we can use the *cluster_centers_* attribute of the KMeans object as shown below:

```
print(km_clus.cluster_centers_
)
```

The output looks like this:

```
[[ 1992.77777778  4394.44444444]
 [ 1983.5         2583.33333333]
 [ 2001.2         6200.        ]]
```

These are the coordinates of the centroids of the three clusters formed by the KMeans clustering algorithm for car_price data.

To find the labels of the different data points, use the labels_ attribute as shown below:

```
print(km_clus.labels_)
```

The output looks like this:

```
[1 1 1 0 0 2 1 2 0 0 1 0 0 2 2 0 0 2 0 1]
```

The three clusters formed by the algorithm have been named 0, 1 and 2. It is important to mention that these cluster names have no mathematical significance and they are there just to name the clusters. If there was another cluster, it would have been labeled as 4.

5. **Plotting the Clusters**

The labels don't given any visual information about the clusters. Therefore, let's plot clusters. Execute the following script:

```
plt.scatter(car_data['Year'],
car_data['Price'],      c      =
km_clus.labels_,
cmap='rainbow')
```

The output looks like this:

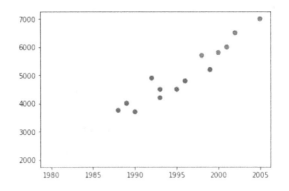

From the output we can see that the clusters formed are according to our expectations. Cars with low price and very old manufacturing year have been clustered together in the(green data points, cars that are average old and have average price have been clustered together (blue data points) and cars with new models and high price have been clustered together (red data points)

Finally, let's see the centroid along with clusters, execute the following script:

```
plt.scatter(car_data['Year'],
car_data['Price'],         c       =
km_clus.labels_,
cmap='rainbow')
plt.scatter(km_clus.cluster_ce
nters_[:,0],km_clus.cluster_ce
nters_[:,1], color='yellow')
```

The output looks like this:

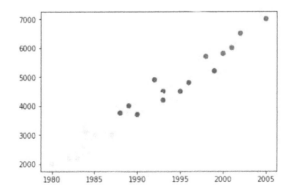

The centroids for each cluster have been displayed in yellow.

Conclusion

In this chapter, we studied a very interesting clustering technique i.e. K-Means clustering. In the next chapter we will study another extremely useful clustering technique i.e. Hierarchical Clustering!

Chapter 15

Hierarchical Clustering

In the last chapter we studied K-Mean clustering which is a type of unsupervised learning. In this chapter we are going to study another clustering technique i.e. Hierarchical Clustering. Clustered formed by hierarchical clustering, can be sometimes similar to the K-Means clustering; however the process of Hierarchical Clustering is quite different. Hierarchical Clustering has two types: Divisive and Agglomerative. In divisive clustering, the data points are initially treated as one big cluster and a top-down approach is followed to divide this one big cluster into several small clusters. On the other hand in Agglomerative clustering involves bottom-up approach. In this chapter, we will cover Agglomerative clustering since it is the most commonly used clustering type.

Hierarchical Clustering Theory

Hierarchical clustering involves following steps:

1. In the beginning every data point is treated as one cluster. Therefore, if there are N data points the total number of clusters at the beginning are N.

2. Join the two closest points, resulting in N-1 clusters.

3. Again join the two closest clusters from to form N-2 clusters.

4. Repeat step 3 until one huge cluster is formed.

5. Use dendrograms to divide one big cluster into required number of clusters. We will study the concept of dendrograms in details

Calculating Cluster Distance

It is important to mention here that there are several ways to find distance between the two clusters and both Euclidean and Manhattan distances can be used for this purpose. Distance between the clusters can be calculated using one of the following ways:

1. Distance between two closest points of the cluster can be calculated.

2. Distance between two farthest points of the cluster can be calculated.

3. Distance between the centroids of two clusters can be calculated.

4. Mean of the distance between all possible combinations of points can be calculated.

Using Dendrograms for Clustering

We said earlier that dendrograms are used to divide one huge cluster into required number of clusters. In this section we will see with the help of an example as to how dendrograms actually work.

Execute the following script:

```
import numpy as np

data = np.array([
    [1992,3000],
    [1995,4000],
    [1998,4500],
    [1996,4200],
    [1999,4700],
    [1993,3500],
```

```
[2001,5700],
[2004,6000],
[2008,6500],
[2005,5800],
[2007,6200],
[2009,6700],])
```

The script above creates a two dimensional list of integers. Consider them car models and corresponding price.

Let's plot these data points. Execute the following script to do so:

```
import   matplotlib.pyplot   as
plt

annots = range(1, 13)
plt.figure(figsize=(12, 8))
plt.subplots_adjust(bottom=0.1
)
plt.scatter(data[:,0],data[:,1
], label='True Position')
```

```
for label, x, y in zip(annots,
data[:, 0], data[:, 1]):
    plt.annotate(
        label,
        xy=(x, y), xytext=(-2,
2),
        textcoords='offset
points',              ha='right',
va='bottom')
plt.show()
```

The data points look like this:

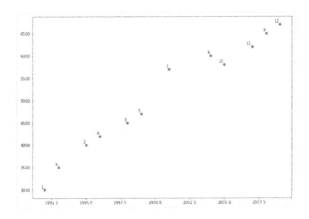

From the first look we can see that point's 1-6 form one cluster and points 7 to 12 form another cluster.

Now let's see how dendrograms are used to form these clusters. Execute the following script to create dendrograms for the above data points.

```
from   scipy.cluster.hierarchy
import dendrogram, linkage
from matplotlib import pyplot
as plt


annot     =     linkage(data,
'single')


marks = range(1, 13)


plt.figure(figsize=(12, 8))
dendrogram(annot,
           orientation='top',
           labels=marks,

distance_sort='descending',
```

```
show_leaf_counts=True)
plt.show()
```

To create the dendrograms we can use the *dendrogram* and *linkage* classes of the *scipy.cluster.hierarchy* library.

The dendrograms generated for the above data points looks like this:

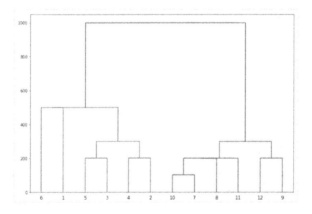

Dendrograms are created following the steps we mentioned earlier. First the two closest points are joined together. These points are depicted at the bottom of the dendrogram hierarchy. For instance points 6 and 1, 5 and 3, 4 and 2, 10 and 7, these points are closest to each other. The vertical height of the point corresponds to Euclidean distance between the points. Finally when the closes points are joined to form clusters, the closest clusters are joined together, for instance cluster of points 5, 3 and 3, 4 have been joined together. This process continues until one big cluster is formed.

Once one large cluster is formed, find longest vertical line with no horizontal line passing through it. Draw a horizontal line through. The number of points at which the horizontal line cross vertical lines, will be the number of clusters.

For instance in the following figure, the dotted black line is the vertical line with longest distance. We drew a red line through this vertical line. The red line cuts two vertical lines resulting in two clusters as shown below:

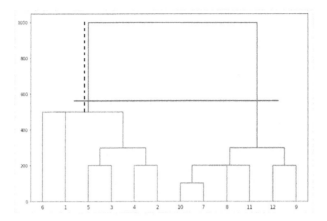

If you look at the points in two clusters, green cluster contains points 1 to 6 while red cluster contains points 7 to 12 as expected.

Hierarchical Clustering with Python Scikit Learn

In the last section we draw dendrograms using Scipy library. However hierarchical clustering can also be implemented using Python's Scikit Learn Library.

The problem that we are going to solve in this section is to cluster the customers into groups based on their spending habits. The data has been downloaded and named as customer_records.csv.

Next, follow these steps to implement hierarchical clustering with Python Scikit Learn:

Importing Libraries

```
import matplotlib.pyplot as plt
import pandas as pd
import numpy as np
%matplotlib inline
```

Importing the Dataset

The following script imports the dataset and stores it in customer_record dataframe

```
customer_record =
pd.read_csv('D:\Datasets\custo
mer_records.csv')
```

To view the dataset, execute the following script:

```
customer_record.head()
```

The output looks like this:

	CustomerID	Genre	Age	Annual Income (k$)	Spending Score (1-100)
0	1	Male	19	15	39
1	2	Male	21	15	81
2	3	Female	20	16	6
3	4	Female	23	16	77
4	5	Female	31	17	40

The dataset has five attributes CustomerID, Genre, Age, Annual Income (In thousand dollars) and Spending Score (1-100). The spending score column corresponds to user spending habits. The more a user spends, the higher is this spending score column. For the sake of simplicity, we will just take two columns i.e. Annual Income and Spending Score and try to cluster our data according to these two columns. To select the two columns, execute the following script:

```
dataset                    =
customer_record.iloc[:,
3:5].values
```

Clustering the Data

To cluster the data using Python's Scikit Learn, we can use the *scipy.cluster.hierarchy* library. It has two classes: *linkage* and

437

dendrogram. First we need to create an object of linkage class and pass the dataset and the distance method to linkage class. Next we need to pass the object of the linkage class to dendrogram class as shown in the following script. Here the distance method used is "ward" which basically minimizes the distance variants between multiple clusters. Execute the following script:

```
import scipy.cluster.hierarchy
as hc


plt.figure(figsize=(12, 8))
plt.title("Customer Clusters")
link   =   hc.linkage(dataset,
method='ward')
dendograms                      =
hc.dendrogram(link)
```

The above script results in the following dendogram chart:

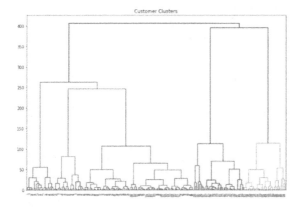

In the above script let's draw a line at 200 at vertical axis. This will give us five clusters as shown in the following figure:

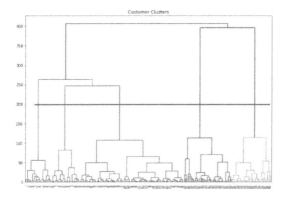

Similarly if you draw horizontal line at 300, the resulting number of cluster will be 3.

Higher threshold results in lesser number of clusters and vice versa.

Conclusion

In this Chapter we studied Hierarchical Clustering which is a very important unsupervised learning technique. With this we will end the unsupervised learning section. In the next Chapter we will study dimensionality reduction techniques i.e. Principal component analysis and Linear Discriminant analysis. Happy Coding!!!

Chapter 16

Dimensionality Reduction with PCA

Machine learning as a discipline has advanced quite a bit in recent years owing to the availability of high performance hardware and storage spaces. Algorithms that use to take months to run 20 years ago can now be run in minutes. Though execution speed of machine learning algorithms has improved significantly, there are still few bottlenecks that slow machine learning algorithms down.

Huge dataset and large number of features per dataset is one of the reasons of slow execution of the algorithms. It is not advisable to reduce number of records from a dataset since they may contain useful information. However, number of features in a dataset can be reduced.

There are two main ways to reduce features in a dataset:

1. Correlated features can be merged resulting in lesser number of features.
2. Choose features that cause maximum variance in the dataset as well as in the output.

The second method is normally preferred and several statistical techniques have been developed in this regard e.g. Factor Analysis, Linear Discriminant Analysis (LDA) and Principal Component Analysis (PCA). In this chapter we will study PCA and in the next chapter we will study LDA.

Principal Component Analysis Theory

Principal component analysis is one of the most widely used techniques for dimensionality reduction. PCA works by selecting features that cause maximum variance in the output, leaving behind features that have no effect on the output. The intuition behind this approach is that variance can be used as a measure for distinguishing output; hence features that are responsible for distinguishing outputs are more important and hence should be selected. First principal component is the feature that results in maximum variance, similarly second principal component is the feature that causes second largest variance and so on.

PCA has two major advantages:

1. Reduced number of features means reduced training time, thus faster execution time.
2. We can only view data in three dimensions; in higher dimensions it is not particularly easy to view the data. With reduced number of features, data can easily be viewed.

It is important to mention here that data must be scaled before applying PCA since variance can be huge for features expressed in higher units such as kilograms, millions, light years etc. Therefore, PCA can be biased towards features these features.

Implementing PCA with Sklearn

In this section, we will see how we can use Python's Scikit Learn library to implement principal component analysis. Using PCA, we will find the most important features from the bank note authentication data. We have four attributes in the dataset i.e. entropy, skewness, variance and curtosis of the wavelet transformed image of the currency note.

More details about the dataset can be found at this link.

The dataset has been supplied with the book and can be found by the name of banknote_data.csv in the Datasets folder. Follow these steps

1- Importing Required Libraries

```
import pandas as pd
import numpy as np
import matplotlib.pyplot as plt
%matplotlib inline
```

2- Importing the Dataset

The following script imports the dataset.

```
banknote_data =
pd.read_csv(r'D:\Datasets\bank
note_data.csv')
```

The script above reads the dataset and stores it in *banknote_data dataframe*.

3- Analyzing the Data

The following script returns the data dimensions:

```
banknote_data.shape
```

The above script returns (1372, 5) which means that our dataset contains 1372 records and five attributes.

To see how the data looks like, execute the following script. It returns the first five rows of the data.

```
banknote_data.head()
```

The output looks like this:

	Variance	Skewness	Curtosis	Entropy	Class
0	3.62160	8.6661	-2.8073	-0.44699	0
1	4.54590	8.1674	-2.4586	-1.46210	0
2	3.86600	-2.6383	1.9242	0.10645	0
3	3.45660	9.5228	-4.0112	-3.59440	0
4	0.32924	-4.4552	4.5718	-0.98880	0

4- Data Preprocessing

To following script divides the data into feature and label set.

```
features=
banknote_data.iloc[:,0:4].valu
es
labels=
banknote_data.iloc[:,4].values
```

Finally let's divide the data into 80 % training and 20% test sets:

```
from sklearn.model_selection
import train_test_split

train_features, test_features,
train_labels, test_labels =
train_test_split(features,
labels, test_size = 0.2,
random_state = 0)
```

5- Scaling the Data

For Random Forest algorithm, it is not necessary to scale the data, however just for the sake of practice, let's scale the data using standard scalar. Remember we discussed scaling in the 3rd chapter.

```python
from sklearn.preprocessing
import StandardScaler

feature_scaler =
StandardScaler()

train_features =
feature_scaler.fit_transform(t
rain_features)

test_features =
feature_scaler.transform(test_
features)
```

6- Applying PCA

It is very easy to implement PCA via sklearn library, we need to use PCA class of the *sklearn.decomposition* library. The number of principal components to select can be passed as parameter to the PCA class. If no number of components is passed, all the features are selected as principal component. Next, we need to call the fit and transform methods and pass them the training and test features. We do not need to pass the output since PCA is an unsupervised learning technique and calculates variance from the feature set alone. Execute the following script to get all the four principal components for the banknote_data.csv dataset.

```
from sklearn.decomposition
import PCA


pca = PCA()
train_features =
pca.fit_transform(train_featur
es)
test_features =
pca.transform(test_features)
```

Now, to see the variance retrieved by each component sorted by descending order, print the *explained_variance_ratio_* attribute on the screen as shown below:

```
exp_var =
pca.explained_variance_ratio_
print(exp_var)
```

The output looks like this:

```
[ 0.54159993  0.32604745  0.08719788  0.04515474]
```

From the output, it can be seen that the first principal component is responsible for 54.15 % variance in the dataset, similarly the second principal component causes 32.60 percent variance in the dataset.

Performance Evaluation with One Principal Component

Let's evaluate how the Random Forest algorithm performs with only one principal component. Repeat the steps 1 to 5 (Not step 6) in the previous section and then execute the following script:

```
pca = PCA(1)
train_features =
pca.fit_transform(train_featur
es)
test_features =
pca.transform(test_features)
```

Now let's train Random Forest algorithm on train features with one principal component and test the algorithm on test features. Execute the following script:

```python
from sklearn.ensemble import
RandomForestClassifier
```

```python
rf_clf =
RandomForestClassifier(n_estim
ators=50, random_state=0)
```

```python
rf_clf.fit(train_features,
train_labels)
```

```python
predictions = rf_clf .predict(
test_features)
```

Finally let's see how well the Random Forest algorithm performs with one principal component. Execute the following script:

```python
from sklearn.metrics import
classification_report,
confusion_matrix,
accuracy_score
```

```python
print(confusion_matrix(test_la
bels, predictions))
```

```python
print(classification_report(te
st_labels, predictions))
```

```python
print(accuracy_score(test_labe
ls, predictions))
```

The output looks like this:

```
[[101  56]
 [ 42  76]]
                precision    recall  f1-score   support

            0        0.71      0.64      0.67       157
            1        0.58      0.64      0.61       118

avg / total        0.65      0.64      0.65       275

0.643636363636
```

With one principal component, the
accuracy achieved is 64.36%.

Performance Evaluation with Two Principal Component

To evaluate, performance with 2 principle
components, execute the following script:

```
pca = PCA(2)
train_features =
pca.fit_transform(train_featur
es)
test_features =
pca.transform(test_features)
from sklearn.ensemble import
RandomForestClassifier


rf_clf =
RandomForestClassifier(n_estim
ators=50, random_state=0)
```

```
rf_clf.fit(train_features,
train_labels)

predictions = rf_clf .predict(
test_features)
```

Finally let's see how well the Random Forest algorithm performs with two principal components. Execute the following script:

```
from sklearn.metrics import
classification_report,
confusion_matrix,
accuracy_score

print(confusion_matrix(test_la
bels, predictions))

print(classification_report(te
st_labels, predictions))

print(accuracy_score(test_labe
ls, predictions))
```

The output looks like this:

```
[[145  12]
 [ 22  96]]
             precision    recall  f1-score   support

          0       0.87      0.92      0.90       157
          1       0.89      0.81      0.85       118

avg / total       0.88      0.88      0.88       275

0.876363636364
```

With two principal components, the accuracy achieved is 87.63%. Similarly, with three and four components the accuracy improves to 98.54% and 99.63%. This shows that the accuracy improvement diminishes after 3 components; therefore 3 components can be retained.

Conclusion

In this chapter, we saw how we can use PCA for dimensionality reduction. In the next chapter, we will see how we can use LDA for dimensionality reduction. Happy Coding!

Chapter 17

Dimensionality Reduction with LDA

In the previous chapter, we saw how what dimensionality reduction is and how we can use Principal Component Analysis (PCA) to reduce number of features in a dataset. In this chapter we will see how we can use LDA for the same purpose.

Linear Discriminant Analysis Theory

LDA is a supervised dimensionality reduction technique which tries to select features based on their ability to distinguish the output. LDA relies on the output of the records as well. Where as in PCA, feature set is enough and labels are not required for feature reduction. As a first step in LDA, related data points are clustered together before being projected into a new dimension where the distance between each cluster is maximized. Similarly, the distance between each data points and its corresponding cluster centroid is minimized.

Implementing LDA with Scikit Learn

In this section we will implement LDA with Python's Scikit Learn library. We will again try to reduce dimensions of the banknote_data.csv dataset. Follow these steps:

1- Importing Required Libraries

```
import pandas as pd
import numpy as np
import matplotlib.pyplot as plt
%matplotlib inline
```

2- Importing the Dataset

The following script imports the dataset.

```
banknote_data =
pd.read_csv(r'D:\Datasets\bank
note_data.csv')
```

The script above reads the dataset and stores it in *banknote_data dataframe*.

3- Analyzing the Data

The following script returns the data dimensions:

```
banknote_data.shape
```

The above script returns (1372, 5) which means that our dataset contains 1372 records and five attributes.

To see how the data looks like, execute the following script. It returns the first five rows of the data.

```
banknote_data.head()
```

The output looks like this:

	Variance	Skewness	Curtosis	Entropy	Class
0	3.62160	8.6661	-2.8073	-0.44699	0
1	4.54590	8.1674	-2.4586	-1.46210	0
2	3.86600	-2.6383	1.9242	0.10645	0
3	3.45660	9.5228	-4.0112	-3.59440	0
4	0.32924	-4.4552	4.5718	-0.98880	0

4- Data Preprocessing

To following script divides the data into feature and label set.

```
features=
banknote_data.iloc[:,0:4].valu
es

labels=
banknote_data.iloc[:,4].values
```

Finally let's divide the data into 80 % training and 20% test sets:

```
from sklearn.model_selection
import train_test_split

train_features, test_features,
train_labels, test_labels =
train_test_split(features,
labels, test_size = 0.2,
random_state = 0)
```

5- Scaling the Data

For Random Forest algorithm, it is not necessary to scale the data, however just for the sake of practice, let's scale the data using standard scalar. Remember we discussed scaling in the 3rd chapter.

```
from sklearn.preprocessing
import StandardScaler

feature_scaler =
StandardScaler()
```

```
train_features =
feature_scaler.fit_transform(t
rain_features)

test_features =
feature_scaler.transform(test_
features)
```

6- Applying PCA

It is very easy to implement PCA via sklearn library, we need to use *LinearDiscriminantAnalysis* class of the *sklearn.discriminant_analysis* library. The *n_components* parameter is used to set the number of linear discriminants. Next, we need to call the fit and transform methods and pass them the training features and training labels. Remember in case of PCA we only needed to pass the feature set and not the labels. Execute the following script to get the first linear discriminant for the dataset.

```
 from
sklearn.discriminant_analysis
import
LinearDiscriminantAnalysis
```

```
LDA =
LinearDiscriminantAnalysis
(n_components=1)
train_features =
LDA.fit_transform(train_featur
es, train_labels)
test_features =
LDA.transform(test_features)
```

Performance Evaluation with One Linear Discriminant

Now let's train Random Forest algorithm on train features with one linear discriminant and test the algorithm on test features. Execute the following script:

```
from sklearn.ensemble import
RandomForestClassifier


rf_clf =
RandomForestClassifier(n_estim
ators=50, random_state=0)
rf_clf.fit(train_features,
train_labels)
```

```
predictions = rf_clf .predict(
test_features)
```

Finally let's see how well the Random Forest algorithm performs with linear discriminant. Execute the following script:

```
from sklearn.metrics import
classification_report,
confusion_matrix,
accuracy_score

print(confusion_matrix(test_la
bels, predictions))

print(classification_report(te
st_labels, predictions))

print(accuracy_score(test_labe
ls, predictions))
```

The output looks like this:

```
[[156   1]
 [  1 117]]
            precision    recall  f1-score   support

         0       0.99      0.99      0.99       157
         1       0.99      0.99      0.99       118

avg / total       0.99      0.99      0.99       275

0.992727272727
```

Here accuracy achieved with 1 linear discriminant i.e. 99.27% is compared to

99.63% achieved by four principal components in last chapter.

Conclusion

In this chapter, we studied LDA in detail. If the data is uniformly distributed LDA will outperform PCA in most cases. However in case of irregular data, PCA performs better. Furthermore PCA can be used with labeled as well as unlabeled data. Happy Coding!!!

Chapter 18

Performance Evaluation with Cross Validation and Grid Search

Welcome to the final chapter of the book. In this chapter we are going to see how we can evaluate performance of an algorithm in a more robust way.

Till now we have been evaluating algorithm performance using by splitting the data into training and test sets and then training the model on the training set and testing it on the test set. However there are certain problems associated with this approach. One such problem is variance. This problem can be solved using Cross Validation.

Another problem that affects the performance comparison of different algorithms is use of various hyper parameters such as K in KNN algorithm and n_estimators in Random Forest algorithm. To compare two algorithms, we need to find the parameters that result in best performance. This problem can be solved using Grid Search algorithm.

In this chapter, we will study Cross Validation and Grid Search in detail.

Cross Validation

Earlier we said that splitting data randomly into training and test set can lead to variance problem. Variance in performance evaluation of an algorithm refers to scenario where an algorithm performance varies depending upon the test set being used.

Cross validation is the solution to variance problem. In cross validation, dataset is divided into K folds where K is any integer. Each of the K folds or partition is at least once used in the training set as well as testing set. For instance let's divide the dataset into 5 partitions. In the first iteration, first 4 partitions are used for training and 5th partition is used as testing. In the second fold, 1,2,3 and 5th partition is used for training and 4th partition is used for testing. In this way every partition is used at least once for testing. The final performance of the algorithm can be evaluated by taking mean of the results from individual tests. This solves variance problem since now the result is based on algorithm being trained and tested on the complete dataset.

Cross Validation with Python's Scikit Learn

The problem that we are going to solve with Random Forest algorithm cross validation is predicting the quality of wine depending upon several features.

More details about the dataset can be found at this link. We will only use the dataset for the red wine. Data has been supplied with the book and can be found in the Datasets folder with name redwine_data.csv.

Follow these steps

7- Importing Required Libraries

```
import pandas as pd
import numpy as np
import matplotlib.pyplot as plt
%matplotlib inline
```

8- Importing the Dataset

The following script imports the dataset.

```
redwine_data =
pd.read_csv(r'D:\Datasets\redw
ine_data.csv', sep=';')
```

The script above reads the dataset and stores it in *banknote_data dataframe*.

9- Data Analysis

To see how the data looks like, execute the following script. It returns the first five rows of the data.

```
redwine_data.head()
```

The output looks like this:

	fixed acidity	volatile acidity	citric acid	residual sugar	chlorides	free sulfur dioxide	total sulfur dioxide	density	pH	sulphates	alcohol	quality
0	7.4	0.70	0.00	1.9	0.076	11.0	34.0	0.9978	3.51	0.56	9.4	5
1	7.8	0.88	0.00	2.6	0.098	25.0	67.0	0.9968	3.20	0.68	9.8	5
2	7.8	0.76	0.04	2.3	0.092	15.0	54.0	0.9970	3.26	0.65	9.8	5
3	11.2	0.28	0.56	1.9	0.075	17.0	60.0	0.9980	3.16	0.58	9.8	6
4	7.4	0.70	0.00	1.9	0.076	11.0	34.0	0.9978	3.51	0.56	9.4	5

10- Data Preprocessing

The following script divides the data into feature and label set.

```
features=
redwine_data.iloc[:,0:11].valu
es

labels=
redwine_data.iloc[:,11].values
```

Since we will be using cross validation and it
will automatically be splitting the data into
training and test set, here using
train_test_split we will a lot all the data to
training_features and set test size to zero
by passing zero to test size variable as
shown below:

```
from sklearn.model_selection
import train_test_split

train_features, test_features,
train_labels, test_labels =
train_test_split(features,
labels, test_size = 0,
random_state = 0)
```

11- Scaling the Data

For Random Forest algorithm, it is not
necessary to scale the data, however just
for the sake of practice, let's scale the data
using standard scalar. Remember we

467

discussed scaling in the 3rd chapter. We will only scale train_features since there is no data in the test_features variable.

```
from sklearn.preprocessing
import StandardScaler

feature_scaler =
StandardScaler()

train_features =
feature_scaler.fit_transform(t
rain_features)
```

12- Cross Validation

To apply cross validation, the first step is to choose the algorithm that you want to use for cross validation. The following script initializes Random Forest classifier with 500 estimators.

```
from sklearn.ensemble import
RandomForestClassifier

rf_clf =
RandomForestClassifier(n_estim
ators=500, random_state=0)
```

To apply cross validation, the *cross_val_score* class of the *sklearn.model_selection* library is used. The classifier, feature set and label set and the number of folds for cross validation are passed as parameter to the *cross_val_score* class as shown below:

```
from sklearn.model_selection
import cross_val_score
rf_accuracies =
cross_val_score(estimator=rf_c
lf, X=train_features, y
=train_labels, cv=5)
```

In the script above, we perform 5 fold cross validation.

To see the accuracies returned by the *cross_val_score* class for all the five folds, you can print the list of values returned by *the cross_val_score* class as follows:

```
print(rf_accuracies)
```

The above script returns following results:

```
[ 0.7173913   0.68224299  0.71028037  0.68867925  0.69085174]
```

469

You can see that accuracies of all the five folds are more or less similar.

To see the average of all the accuracies, you can call mean() function on the list as shown below:

```
print(rf_accuracies.mean())
```

The result shows: 0.69788 i.e. 69.788%.

Finally to see the standard deviation, execute the following script:

```
print(rf_accuracies.std())
```

The above script returns 0.0135 or 1.35% which is very less. Therefore we can say that our dataset has very less variance and results obtained on all the sets are can be considered correct and close to the average.

Gird Search for Parameter Selection

Job of a machine learning algorithm is to find best set of parameters or weights that yield best results. These parameters are found by the algorithms and depend upon the dataset. We cannot control these parameters.

However there is another set of parameters that is specified before the algorithm is run. For instance value of K for the KNN algorithm, the type of kernel for the SVM algorithm, the number of estimators for the Random forest algorithm, number of nodes for the neural network and so on. These parameters can be controlled or specified.

However we do not really know the best value for these parameters. In the last section we set the n_estimator for the Random Forest algorithm to 500. However we do not know if this is the ideal. What if the algorithm performs better with 200 or 700 nodes? OR what is the best value of K? 10 Or 20? We do not know the answer to these questions.

Grid Search algorithm helps us solve this problem. Basically what Grid Search algorithm does is, it automatically finds best parameters for a particular algorithm from a set of parameters.

Implementing Grid Search with Sklearn

The Python's Scikit Learn library comes with a package to implement Grid Search. For this purpose the sklearn.model_selection class contains GridSearchCV class that can be used to implement Grid Search. However before that some preprocessing is required.

Creating Parameter Dictionary

Grid search algorithm doesn't just randomly run and finds all the best parameters for an algorithm because it can take years. For instance if grid search algorithm starts testing each value for the number of estimators parameter from 1 to 1000, the algorithm has to run a minimum of 1000 times and that's just for 1 parameter. Therefore a set of values for each parameter that you want to test, is passed to the GridSearchCV class. These set of parameters and are expressed in the form of a dictionary.

Suppose we want to test different values for n_estimators, warm_start and criterion parameters of the Random Forest algorithm, we can create a dictionary that looks like this:

```
param = {
    'n_estimators': [100, 250,
500, 750, 1000],
    'warm_start': ['True',
'False'],
    'criterion': ['entropy',
'gini']
}
```

In the script above we create a dictionary named, "param" the keys for the dictionary are the names of the parameters and the values of the dictionary corresponds to values of the parameter. From these set of values, the Grid Search algorithm will return the best combination.

For instance we want to test the best value for n_estimators parameter and we passed 100, 250, 500, 750 and 1000. Grid search will select best value from these five values. It is important to mention here that grid search algorithm can take lot of time depending upon the values that you want to test and the number of folds for the cross validation.

For instance in our case we have 5 values for n_estimators parameter, 2 values for warm_start and two values for criterion. Total possible combinations in this case are 5 x 2 x 2 = 20. Multiply this value with number of folds e.g 5. That makes it 100 executions. This can slow down the algorithm a bit.

Creating Parameter Dictionary

To execute the Grid Search, we need create object of GridSearchCV class and pass it the classifier (we will use Random Forest classifier created in the last section), the parameter dictionary that we just created, the performance evaluation metrics (we will use accuracy), cross validation folds and the number of jobs. When n_jobs = -1, it means that all the CPU's should be used for performing Grid Search. Execute the following script to create GridSearch object.

```
from sklearn.model_selection
import GridSearchCV
grid_search =
GridSearchCV(estimator=rf_clf,

param_grid=param,

scoring='accuracy',
                      cv=5,
                      n_jobs=-
1)
```

The final step is to call fit method on the GridSearchCV object and pass it the training and test set as shown below:

```
grid_search.fit(train_features
, train_labels)
```

This can take a bit of time to execute.

Once the above script executes, the last and final step is to see the parameters selected by grid search, to do so you can use the best_params_ attribute of the GridSearchCV class as shown below:

```
optimal_parameters =
grid_search.best_params_
print(optimal_parameters)
```

The output looks like this:

```
{'criterion': 'gini', 'n_estimators': 750, 'warm_start': 'True'}
```

Best achieved with aforementioned parameters values. Finally to see the accuracy achieved using most optimal parameters, execute the following script:

```
 optimal_results =
grid_search.best_score_
print(optimal_results)
```

Conclusion

With this chapter, this book comes to its end. From here on I would suggest you to study machine learning on your own. Following are some of the very good resources:

1. For Python: https://www.python.org/
2. For Machine Learning: http://scikit-learn.org/stable/
3. For Deep Learning: https://keras.io/
4. For datasets: https://archive.ics.uci.edu/ml/index.php

FREE E-BOOK DOWNLOAD :

http://bit.ly/2yJsyq4

or

http://pragmaticsolutionstech.co
m/

Use the link above to get instant access
to the bestselling E-Book **Data
Analytics' Guide For Beginners**

.